EVANGELIZATION AND POLITICS

Addresses and related papers from an
International Meeting of Theologians
held at the Evangelical Seminary of
Theology, Matanzas, Cuba, February
25–March 2, 1979.

editors: Sergio Arce Martinez
Oden Marichal Rodriguez

The original Spanish published by
the Evangelical Seminary of
Theology, 1981. The English
translation published by the New
York CIRCUS, Inc., 1982.

Translators: Richard Post
David J. Kalke

Martha Blume

Information on bulk order discounts is available upon request.
Please direct inquiries and orders to:
New York CIRCUS, Inc.
P. O. Box 37
Times Square Station
New York, New York 10108

TABLE OF CONTENTS

*   *   *

EVANGELIZATION

AND

POLITICS

Dedicated to the Memory of

FATHER ALEX MORELLI
(1919-1979)

A BIOGRAPHICAL SKETCH

OF

FATHER ALEX MORELLI

(1919 - 1979)

Alex Morelli was born in Marseilles, France, near Jean
Juarés Square, February 25, 1919. At the age of seventeen
he entered the Dominican Order, beginning his novitiate on
September 14 and making his profession of vows one year later.
He studied at the Theological Seminary of San Maximo, France.
Because of the Second World War his ordination was moved up
to June 28, 1942, the Feast of Saint Irene. Ordination at
this time enabled him to begin as a worker-priest volunteer-
ing in chaplaincies that had been secretly organized in German work camps in Dusseldorf. These camps had been organized
in response to a call made by the French bishops.

After working there for two months as a worker-priest in
what he described as "impassioned labor," he was discovered
by the Nazi Gestapo. On August 28, 1943, he was imprisoned.
For the next seven months he lived under atrocious conditions
in solitary confinement, in a tiny cell, awaiting trial. Then
he was taken to the sadly celebrated concentration camp of
Dachau, one kilometer from Munich, where he was kept for two
years. He lived through an incredible experience of faith
with an intensive dedication to others, to whom he dedicated
his book LAND OF DISTRESS, published in 1947.

When liberation came on April 30, 1945, he went directly
to his mother in Marseilles to show her that he was alive.
Twenty-four hours later he returned to Germany to attend the
ill and agonizing persons who had to remain there because of
their precarious condition. He stayed there and worked for
three months.

In 1946 he was appointed Prior of the Convent of Marseilles for six years; and in 1953, with the same title, he
became President of the Convent of Toulouse for six years.
In 1959 he went to Uruguay as a Provincial Vicar. There he
founded the Movement for Independent Action, later called

International Movement for Action in Independent Social Resources (Movimiento Internacional de Acción en los Medios
Sociales Independientes- MIAMSI). He founded branches of
MIAMSI in Brazil and Argentina. Their success has lasted to
this day.

At that time he also worked with the Catholic Worker
Action (Acción Católica Obrera - ACO) and with the Workers'
Movement for Catholic Action (Movimiento Obrero de Acción
Católica - MOAC) in Chile.

He had difficulties with the Papal Nuncio in Uruguay in
1965. Later he returned to France and remained in the Spiritual Center of his Order in San Beaumé.

He arrived in Vera Cruz, Mexico, on September 18, 1967.
There he worked until November 4, 1968, with students at
university cultural centers, but his concern of greatest
priority was the marginal and oppressed. Therefore very
soon after his arrival in Mexico he began work with Father
Pedro Valazquez, in the Social Secretariat of Mexico. In a
few years he became director of its review journal CONTACTO,
which attained great influence throughout Latin America. By
this time his identification with Latin America became the
central focus of his life.

Following the tragedy of Tlateloco he went to the suburb Ahizotla near Mexico City. There he spent three years
as a living testimony working with and for the poorest sector
of Mexicans. Beginning November 4, 1968, he associated with
Padre Rodolfo Escamilla, who was later assassinated for his
devotion to the marginals of Mexico.

In 1972 he wrote a new book, LIBERA A MI PUEBLO, presenting a Latin American perspective of the theology of liberation. The same year he was invited to Netza by the Jesuits
with whom he spent two years. In Netza he was in charge of
the Chapel of San Martin de Porres.

In 1974 he became established in Colonia Central, Mexico, where he pursued and intensified his labors as pastor,
educator and promoter of conscientization, to which he remained faithfully committed until his death. On June 22,
1976, he was diagnosed as having bone cancer. He returned to
France for surgery but returned to Mexico in 1978 on learning
that the cancer would soon prove fatal.

Alex Morelli then started working at CENCOS (National
Center for Social Communication) directed by José Alvarez

Icaza. There he found "a work team after his heart."

In December of 1978 his condition became worse, moving to other parts of his body. Nevertheless, he never ceased working - in the community of Netzahualcoyotl, in Colonia Central and with CENCOS.

At CENCOS he headed the international division and collaborated in publishing notes, editorials, analyses and reviews on various topics. He entered several debates in the press, promoting socialism and the dialogue between Christians and Marxists, to which he gave high priority at this time.

In Netzahualcoyotl he innovated various social work programs while continuing with special zeal his work as priest. Then, before retiring, he organized a cooperative, "Hands of Mexico," to promote the sales of clothing articles made by dressmakers in the neighborhood.

In 1978 he journeyed to Prague to attend the Fifth General Assembly of the Christian Peace Conference. A few months prior to this he attended the First Plenary Assembly of the Latin American and Caribbean division of the Christian Peace Conference.

Early in 1979 he visited Cuba to attend the International Meeting of Theologians. "The best theological meeting I have attended in all my life," he said upon his return.

During Holy Week of 1979 he was hospitalized with intense pain, which he bore courageously. He left the hospital to celebrate his last Mass with his people of Netza at Easter.

Following a slight improvement he returned to France, hoping to prolong his life a bit more. Upon departure he lamented being unable to visit Nicaragua to serve in the Sandinista forces as chaplain. Prior to his death, he completed a manuscript describing his life as a priest, his activities - religious, cultural, social and political - and his ever increasing commitment to the poor and oppressed.

(The above data were taken from CENCOS Bulletin, August, 1979).

*   *   *

SPECIAL INTRODUCTION

TO THE ENGLISH EDITION

EVANGELIZATION AND POLITICS

ROBERT MCAFEE BROWN

Question: What relevance does a conference held in Cuba in 1979 have for North Americans in 1982, 1983, 1984?

Answer: More and more. The issues raised then are even more critical now. Crises are intensifying rather than going away. World perspectives, such as the conference represented, are desperately needed.

This book contains the papers given at a conference rather different from the conferences most North Americans attend. North Americans and Europeans did not dominate, but were a tiny handful of the 78 delegates. Sponsorship was not by mainline churches but by the Latin American and Caribbean Christian Peace Conference. The conference was not held in the United States or Europe, but in Cuba at the Evangelical Seminary in Matanzas. Most of the delegates did not speak out of the ambiance of acceptance of capitalism, but out of acceptance of some form of socialism (and the forms varied) as the economic and political counterpart of the New Testament Gospel. Indeed, the point of greatest similarity to conventional church conferences was the tiny percentage of women delegates - a fact remarked on with considerable vigor by the women present.

The theme was "Evangelization and Politics." It is interesting that it was the delegates from North America (James Cone and myself), who felt independently called upon to make the case that politics and evangelization belong together. From the situation out of which the rest of the delegates came, such association could be taken for granted; it was the nature of the relationship that was explored.

All of this suggests some benefits for North American readers who study these pages. One of them is the importance of being open to points of view that seem initially different from our own. We need to discover why many Christians do affirm a socialist option, and why for them it makes more sense

than Christians elsewhere affirming a capitalist option. We
need to hear Christians who speak out of the context of living in the midst of the poor and disadvantaged, rather than
(as is so often the case with us) hearing Christians talk
about the poor. We need to overhear conversations in which
it is taken for granted that the God of the Bible shows a
partiality for the poor, and discover how such a reading of
the Bible poses new problems for us, the non-poor.

Another advantage of reading these pages is to discover
how much we have in common with those from whom we seem so
separated. The conference engaged in daily Bible study, under the leadership of Adolfo Ham, a Cuban seminary professor
and pastor. The conclusions of other Christian gatherings
were continually cited, especially the meeting of evangelical Protestants at Oaxtapec just a few months earlier, and
the meeting of the Latin American Roman Catholic Bishops in
Puebla just a few weeks earlier. Much discussion centered
around key concepts in Christian experience such as salvation,
the role of the Church, evangelization, the place of individual experience, and so on. While some things (from a North
American perspective) were done with these themes, the themes
themselves are ones with which all Christians can resonate,
and a discussion is possible even in the midst of differences.
(Let it be recorded that there were differences within the
conference itself.) There was no theological or political
"party line" to which all were expected to adhere. (The speech
of Metropolitan Gregorios is sufficient evidence of this, as
were some of the spirited exchanges on the floor of the conference, notably one between James Cone and Hugo Assmann).

A third advantage of such exposure is that it helps
us to get rid of many stereotypes we bring to examinations
of "third world Christians," or advocates of "liberation
theologies." It is important that we hear adherents of such
positions on their own terms rather than through the distorted interpretations of certain North American detractors.
Particularly significant is the way these essays give the lie
to the notion that third world theology is "mere politics,"
or "thinly veiled Marxism," or "a repudiation of the Church
in the name of class struggle"- to cite only a few of the
caricatures typical of insecure North American Christians.
The very insistence of the conference that politics cannot
be separated from evangelization gives the lie to most of

8

these assertions. This is not to deny that there is economic analysis, employment of Marx, and acknowledgement of class struggle. But they are seen in the context of the Christian Gospel. Class struggle, for example, a phrase that causes most North Americans to shudder, is not seen here as a formula or code word, but as a simple description of what goes on in the world when perceived from the vantage point of the poor. For them life is struggle, little else, and they cannot help noticing that the people who are making their struggle for survival necessary are the rich and powerful, members, indeed, of another "class" in society. Karl Marx did no invent class struggle; he simply noticed it and reported what he saw. Christians who are victims of the class struggle do not desire to perpetuate it but to overcome it, so that it will no longer describe the world, and so that instead of exploitation and starvation being the lot of the majority of people on earth, their lot will be a situation of justice and love - a description not too far from the Biblical understanding of the Kingdom of God.

A fourth advantage of reading these papers is to learn how much of themselves some Christians are willing to put on the line for the sake of their beliefs. The brief account of Father Morelli is only a particularly vivid instance of the commitment to the poor that is the stuff out of which the church's future must be built. On every occasion of decision he could have opted for a more comfortable alternative, and refused to do so. The same is true of Augusto Cotto, one of the guiding lights in the planning and execution of the conference, who later died in an airplane accident of somewhat unclear cause. His was also a life of commitment to the poor like so many thousands in Latin America who commit themselves to the poor and turn up prematurely dead. And for every Morelli and Cotto there are thousands who quietly and heroically jeopardize their own safety for the sake of a cause they believe in - preparing the way for the Kingdom of God by identification with the poor and disadvantaged. Most of them have names we will never know. But those with whom they identify know, and revere them.

A fifth reason to study these speeches is that they remind us that history does not stand still. They help us to see what is happening today from a fresh perspective. Occasionally the news is good. The revolution in Nicaragua was

9

still underway while the conference was meeting. The successful overthrow of the Somoza forces has since been accomplished, and the Sandinistas, peopled by their share of
priests, sisters and laypersons, have an opportunity to establish a new society in which "evangelization and politics"
go hand in hand.

But for the most part, the news is bad. Baleful as many
people thought the Carter Administration was back in 1979 when
the conference was held, at least it had made a more than
token commitment to work for human rights, particularly in
the dictatorial regimes so consistently supported by U.S.
military, political and economic aid. But with the advent of
the Reagan Administration, not only has there been an about
face of U.S. concern for human rights, typified by the callous
remarks of General Haig and Jeanne Kirkpatrick, but there has
been an increasingly militant and hostile attitude toward all
governments, regimes and organizations perceived by Washington
as being "leftist." This has meant throwing massive military
and economic weight against Nicaragua, against attempts at a
peoples' revolution in El Salvador, and (in consistency with
five administrations) against all things Cuban - a piece of political shortsightedness especially deplorable to those who
have been to Cuba and have seen what Cuba has accomplished
since the overthrow of Batista, in spite of an economic blockade by the United States for over twenty years.

All of this makes the attention given at the conference
to the arms race particularly pertinent, since the flip side
of the "anti-communist" coin is always a beefing up of armaments, both those manufactured for use by the United States
and those manufactured to sell to "friendly," i.e. right-
wing nations.

A final reason for interest in these pages is to take
seriously the message of the conference as a whole. If I
dare to paraphrase it in a sentence, it is the theme that
pervades the final report: evangelization in our time is going
to proceed from the periphery to the center.

This is not language that is part of the daily life of
North American Christians, but it is language to which we had
better begin to listen. In the past, evangelization went
from the self-defined "center," i.e. Europe and North America,
out to the edges of human civilization, the "periphery," to
the heathen, non-white, powerless. There were donors and

and there were recipients, and after all the giving and receiving, it was still pretty clear where the power lay. The
donors gave away nothing that threatened their superiority.
But now, the conference report suggests, that movement is
being reversed. If the Good News of the Gospel is Good News
to the poor, then it is the poor, those on the periphery, out
on the edges, who are going to have to be the transmitters
of that Gospel to the rest of us, the non-poor at the center.
This will mean a new understanding of missions, of the Church,
of evangelization and politics; in short, a new understanding
of the Gospel. The speeches suggest some of the dimensions
of that new understanding.

     With very few steps, let us "walk through" some of the
themes that are of special importance to North Americans, not
as an excuse to read no further, but as a whetting of the ap-
petite to read more carefully.
     Sergio Arce, rector of the Evangelical Seminary at Ma-
tanzas that hosted the conference, gave both the opening and
closing speeches. Arce, who had some of this theological
training in the United States, was one of a small band of
Cuban clergy who, when the revolution took place in 1959, did
not leave Cuba, but returned from graduate work to stay and
work there. His speech reflects things learned through twenty years of being part of the first successful socialist revolution in our hemisphere. His talk is tightly knit, and
the sequence is significant. Evangelization he defines as
the esse (the very being) of the Church, and it means reaching out toward and involving the poor (as Jesus said so well
at Nazareth). Politics, in turn, is the esse of evangelization. Arce is particularly helpful in reminding us that the
question, "Which comes first, reflection or action?" is a non-
question, or at least a chicken-and-egg question. The important thing is to see the mutual need of each for the other.
He develops that mutuality in three ways: the need for mutual
generation and stimulation, making the important point that
there is no such thing as the liberation of the individual
alone; the need for mutual control, i.e. ongoing examination
and review of what we are doing, and recognizing that in different contexts we may need to do different things; and the
need for mutual verification, in the literal sense of the word,
i.e. making the truth, embodying the truth, not simply announcing it. The richness of this speech alone would justify

11

the production of the entire volume.

Bishop de Carvahlo of Angola, in a presentation as brief as Arce's is extended, offers an important message for North American Christians that has seldom been put so tersely. He describes the impact of missions on his own people as one that brought capitalist culture along with it, and stresses the need for indigenous peoples (not only in Angola, but everywhere) to shed the colonialism and imperialism that came along with the Gospel, and was for so long thought to be inseparable from it. "To evangelize...means to rediscover the social dimension of the Gospels." (In the ellipsis are the words, "in the meaning of the building of a new Angolan society," but we can affirm the need for this in every cultural situation).

The Rev. Ilsegret Fink, speaking from the East German situation, makes a clear connection between anti-communist propaganda and the arms race, words that need to be heard more clearly in the United States in 1982 and 1983 than they did even in 1979. Her self-critical appraisal of the Church in her country can also be a model for the rest of us, for she distinguishes a trait, common elsewhere but seldom acknowledged, that the churches have too long been conditioned in their whole approach by the ideology of western capitalism. There must be a critique by the Church of an "-ism," but until we are aware of our captivity to our own particular "-ism," we are not likely to be able to see our situation as it truly is.

Because the conference took place at a time when Viet Nam was being invaded by mainland China, François Houtart, a Roman Catholic sociologist, was asked to give a history of the Vietnamese people with special attention to the role of the Church. For our purposes, the important thing in this essay is to note how the United States backed not only the forces of reaction but of repression. Discussion today of our own involvement in El Salvador as "another Viet Nam," in which we are replicating the mistakes of two decades ago, only underlines the timeliness of the analysis.

The intervention of Metropolitan Gregorios of India, as earlier noted,provides a good example of how differences of theological approach can be present within an overall commitment to the poor and dispossessed. The Metropolitan wishes to stress the cultural contributions that can be made to liberation causes. And he is openly sceptical of any marriage between Marxism and Christianity. And yet even in his forthright piece there are interesting points of potential convergence. Gustavo Gutierrez and others have been making a careful study of "popular religion," i.e. the religion of the people, in Latin America, in order that an authentic theology "of the people" can emerge; and the Metropolitan's strong emphasis on the importance of small groups within the churches taking up matters the Church as a whole is not yet ready to face, has its Latin American counterpart in the tens of thousands of comunidades de base on the subcontinent.

The themes of Bishop de Carvahlo receive new urgency in Ernle Gordon's well-documented case study of how imperialism and the Gospel got intertwined in the Caribbean, to the detriment of the Gospel and the people it was trying to serve. His essay, and particularly the materials quoted in it, are even more important today than when first presented, now that President Reagan has unleashed a program for "help" to the Caribbean nations that will make them more than ever dependent on United States capital and subservient to United States wishes. The six points with which the article closes are a fine summation of emphases needed in the immediate future.

Georges Casalis, doughty warrior from France in the interests of social change, stresses how the initiative has moved from the first and second worlds to the third - an important message for northern hemisphere Christians. His dreary report on what capitalism has done to western Europe shows how religion has been a tool to reinforce right-wing responses to crisis, and how such alliances will lead, in the northern as well as the southern hemisphere, to the kind of "national security" state in which the Church will once again find itself in an unholy alliance with repression. For Casalis, for the other speakers, evangelization means taking sides, opting for the poor, in response to the Gospel and in defiance of the mores of the surrounding society.

James Cone describes Black counterparts in North America to the liberation struggles being waged elsewhere. He is harsh in his condemnation of North American whites whom he perceives as looking elsewhere (especially to Latin America) to avoid confronting the basic liberation struggle being waged by Blacks on their own soil. (As one who was an identifiable target of this attack, I do not feel that I should

1 3

use the priivlege of this extra space for rebuttal, and my own
essay, which follows his, but was written without knowledge
of his, will have to serve as the statement of a white North
American trying to confront the liberation struggle on all
fronts).

Perhaps Cone's most important contribution is his own
growing awareness, reflected in his speech, that the Black
struggle, in addition to being a racial struggle, is an economic and international struggle as well. "Faith," he writes,
"must connect itself with a social theory of change." The
importance of economic analysis made its way into Black theology, as he reports, only about two years before the Cuba
conference, and it is an advance that links Black theology
more firmly with other liberation struggles throughout the
world. Cone also made a contribution by stressing the importance of eschatology to the liberation struggle – a much
neglected theme at the conference. As noted earlier, one
of the most spirited exchanges was sparked by this, as Hugo
Assmann, a Brazilian theologian, challenged the relevance
of what Cone called the "transcendence factor" in an understanding of salvation. Cone's drawing on his own tradition
for this emphasis exemplifies the way in which different
theologies contribute to the creation of a more mature overall position.

Reference has already been made to the "Final Document,"
produced, as all "final documents" at conferences are, in
late night sessions, a multiplicity of drafts and frequent
clash of viewpoints. Perhaps for that very reason it serves
as a good summation of the themes of the conference. That
the document is set squarely in the context of earlier conferences of other groups of Christians in Latin America at
Oaxtapec and Puebla, is an important sign of the fact that
continuity and context are taken seriously. The theme of
evangelization moving from the periphery toward the center
is present in a number of places, and the forthright stress
on the Gospel as showing a partiality for the poor is also
constant. Rather than remaining content with generalities,
the document is quite specific in describing what, in a world
of inequality and injustice, the Gospel must embody, not
least in "countries of the center" when Christians seek
to be in solidarity with those on the periphery:

Evangelization is soliciting these objectives: denunciation of the economy of exploitation which subjects people in under-developed countries to capitalism; solidarity actions with refugees and with
political and economic exiles; contribution to a
worldwide public opinion against dictators; boycott against transnational corporations which exploit countries of the periphery; the struggle
against attempts to revive the cold war and widening arms race; efforts to eradicate racism and
sexism...

All in all, an agenda sufficiently comprehensive to
keep us busy and in trouble.

Robert McAfee Brown
Professor of Theology and Ethics
Pacific School of Religion
Delegate to the conference

August, 1982

INTRODUCTION

In this publication we offer to all our fraternal colleagues, especially those of Latin America and the Caribbean,
materials coming out of the International Meeting of Theologians held at the Evangelical Seminary of Theology in Matanzas, Cuba, February 25 - March 2, 1979. The conference was
held on the occasion of the second meeting of the Continuation   Committee of the Latin American and Caribbean Christian Peace Conference. This gathering of celebrated theologians was sponsored by the Latin American and Caribbean
Christian Peace Conference, the Christian Movement for Peace,
Independence and Progress of People and the Evangelical Seminary of Theology.

More than one hundred Christians from around the world
attended the conference. All were committed in one way or
another to the theological task related to discussion and
dialogue on the theme EVANGELIZATION AND POLITICS. The
participants brought with them a wide range of perspectives
and view points on the theme.

It is interesting to note that three of the Christian
traditions were represented: Roman Catholic, Protestant and
Orthodox. The presence of one Roman Catholic Bishop, two
Protestant Bishops and one Metropolitan reflected the importance of the ecumenical aspect of the meeting.

Even though a majority of the attenders were Latin
Americans, an atmosphere of internationalism was created by
the presence of theologians from developing capitalist
countries, from socialist Eastern Europe and from other
countries of the developing world.

It is important to note that the participation of women
and of laypersons was relatively low. Only 10% of the participants were women and about 20% were laypersons.

All of the participants had received theological training in one form or another as a part of their educational experience. Not all were professors nor teachers of theology.
For some theology had not been their primary area of study.
Some were sociologists, psychologists, pastors, religious
workers, social workers, workers, journalists, economists or
university professors in a variety of disciplines.

Four religious publications were represented by their several directors. The participants have published, in total, over one hundred books on theology.

For the Church and for theology in Cuba, the meeting had extraordinary significance. Never before in the history of the Church in Cuba had there been an event of this nature, unique for its ecumenism and internationalism. The criminal blockade placed against our people over twenty years ago by the imperialist government of the United States has separated us spiritually and objectively from the rest of the world. Hence, this meeting took on yet another level of importance not only for Cubans but for all our brothers and sisters who shared the experiences of these meetings. The ecumenism and internationalism of such a meeting cannot be ignored, neither in Cuba nor outside of Cuba.

It is our privilege to publish in this book some general information about the meetings, the Final Document, the Resolutions and the Statements adopted by the general plenaries. The Opening Remarks and Greetings are also included.

Unfortunately we are unable to publish any of the informal discussion which took place during the plenary meetings and meetings of smaller groups, which were extraordinarily productive. We hope nevertheless that our modest efforts in publishing this material may be of some use to the contemporary Church, as it embarks upon one of the most arduous and difficult tasks which it has ever faced in history.

*   *   *

COMMUNICATION

OF

BISHOP KÁROLY TÓTH

Bishop Tóth is the President of the Christian Peace Conference

(Prague, February 22, 1979). I consider it a great privilege to greet the representatives of the Latin American and Caribbean Christian Peace Conference who are attending this important theological meeting, and the Continuation Committee, all of whom are gathered in Matanzas, Cuba. I say this in the name of the entire Christian Peace Conference.

We firmly believe that the Christian Peace Conference in Latin America and the Caribbean has an enormous contribution to make. We have no doubt that the success of the present meeting of theologians will open new avenues for the Christian Peace Conference and will have a vital influence throughout Latin America. We are convinced that the Christian Peace Conference in Latin America and the Caribbean, with its steady growth, will be able to establish guide lines and develop a revolutionary fervor, such as is the essence of Christian evangelism, for the liberation of the people of Latin America.

I must confess that the Church has often erred by endeavoring to withdraw Christianity from the political, sociological and historical arenas of the real world. It has overly spiritualized itself and severed the roots which Jesus Christ established through His Incarnation. The Church tries to live separated from the true world which Christ is saving. The Church tries to live in an unreal world of intellectual attitudes and beliefs. But Christianity does reveal itself historically and concretely. It can be understood and practiced only in this light.

Whenever a crisis arises, the question should never be, "What do the Scriptures say about such and such a situation?" But rather, the question should be, "What does this situation tell us in relation to our interpretation and practice of the Scriptures?" The situation in Latin America is clear. Oppression of various types and the constant struggle for liberation serve to deepen our theological anxieties.

Of course such a realistic interpretation of a situation in which there are Scriptural emergencies will oblige us Christians to cooperate with all groups, parties and organizations which are actively committed to the tasks of liberation. Without fear and with unquenchable valor we must cooperate with all who are fully dedicated to this goal, with the firm realization that no one faction alone can achieve the liberation and peace for which we yearn, and that unless we all strive in complete solidarity, our cause will be in grave danger.

The Christian Peace Conference in Latin America and the Caribbean is one of the paths for the forces of liberation on this continent. It can be said that if we are conscious of our situation and practice our faith under complete control of the Scriptures, a new era can be launched for our sisters and brothers of the area. We must seek and maintain a strict solidarity and unity with all those who are committed to the task of liberation.

In the name of the International Christian Peace Conference, I wish every success for the labors of these theological meetings, and that the meetings may become a memorable event.

Bishop Károly Tóth

*   *   *

INAUGURAL ADDRESS

BY

AUGUSTO COTTO

Rev. Augusto Cotto was a member of the Theological Commission of the Latin American and Caribbean Christian Peace
Conference at the time he gave the following address.

Esteemed Brothers and Sisters, Compañeros and Compañeras,
in Christ's ministry:

The time and the place of this International Meeting of
Theologians are of singular historic importance. Many theological meetings and conferences have taken place in history,
and some of them have witnessed significant advances in the
development of theological thinking. Many of us who are assembled here, in one way or another, have been a part of that
progress. We have offered our share of interest, of hope and
of understanding. A majority of those meetings have been regional and some, in the past, have pretended to represent the
universal nature of theology. But these meetings, through
various defects and limitations, have failed to attain their
desired objectives. They have continued to serve a theology
of domination. Our theological colleagues in Europe and the
United States can attest to this fact.

Without meaning to be arrogant, and without wanting to
freeze the phenomena of history in this moment that we are
gathered here, I boldly predict that with your coming here
as we approach the end of the decade of the seventies, the
Latin American theology of liberation is setting a new
course for the method of doing theology. The basic premise
of this method is not theological discourse in and of itself.
Rather it begins with analysis of the realities of society.
We can say that theology becomes an intellectual statement
or an abstraction of faith beginning from historical and political praxis. On one hand the reality of Latin America
is such that it has been an underdeveloped continent, one
that is exploited and dependent. Yet the sustenance for
understanding our Christian faith has been the academic faith
of the developed lands of the west. These two combine

21

themselves into a cultural medium for the conception of and
for the living of a faith which is militant and challenging.
An evangelical faith which seeks to build the Kingdom of
Heaven on this earth in terms of peace, with just relations
between people and nations is being born in our midst.

If we understand and accept that aspirations for justice
exist, then the theology of liberation includes the aim of
being a universal, an international theology. It has no altars of nationalism nor regional barbarism. We cannot believe that here on the Latin American subcontinent we can
think of truth for the whole world merely because we are one
of the regions most badly damaged by the disorder of the international division of labor, which is one of the most omi-
nous results of capitalism. I do not attach adjectives here
to "capitalism," but merely speak of "capitalism" which engenders misery, oppression and injustice.

Of course, the theology of liberation requires overcoming some aspects not properly within the theoretical
boundaries traditionally assigned to the discipline of
"theology." Many of the assumptions of the theology of
liberation lie within the agreements and persuits of its
projects. That is, many of its concepts are based in a true
commitment to the objectives which it defends. We should not
occupy ourselves so much with new, profitless theories of
elitist thinking. Rather, we should concern ourselves with
mobilizing practices which spring from simple practices of
faith – which, when they take over and unfurl the popular ban-
ners of liberation, convert themselves into heralds for announcing ever better plans for struggle and organizational
actions of the people. It is this aspect of the theology of
liberation – we should call it "pastoral liberation" – which
overcomes the vices of an intellectual ghetto, confined in
cloistered study centers, which go no further than preparing
theological frauds.

These meetings should help us overcome this crisis and
give us a qualitative leap forward towards acquiring a dynamic, dialectic faith such that, with no concrete political
commitment, we shall not have to speak of making a "theology
of liberation."

We have already noted that this International Meeting
of Theologians is historic as to place and time. It is taking place in Cuba, the first socialist state in America, a

status which should be followed of course by other countries. The new theology of Cuba departs fundamentally from the commitment of other believing Christians because of the revolutionary and humanizing process of this heroic people under the leadership of Fidel Castro - whom I do not hesitate in recognizing as one of the most faithful, just and illustrious men of the twentieth century. The theology of Cuba is a theology which one cannot lay aside, as we said at the Conference of Theologians we held in Mexico in October of 1977.

The present meetings are historical furthermore because of their timing. The change in the balance of forces in the world presents us with new challenges. In this respect we cannot speak of past decades and years; but we must now speak of months and weeks. In Central America the struggle against traditional tyrannies in recent months has become bloody. The popular uprising in Nicaragua against a dictatorship and his Praetorian forces gives us a ray of hope for prompt changes. Guatemala and El Salvador, defended by their solid mass organizations, are in turn starting their final conflict against dictatorships. Mass organizations in El Salvador have been able to prevent the establishment of a fascist model which might have become the first victory of true fascism, structurally conceived, in Latin America.

These revolutionary forces in El Salvador have been able to isolate the governing military clique of the oligarchial fraction of the bourgeoisie to such a point that in their desperation they had to establish an emergency regime. This regime legitimated itself through a decree sadly known as the "Law to Guarantee and Defend the Public Order," so as to reign not through reason but through terror.

The victory of the Cambodian people is a victory over the macabre "Chinaization" of Southeastern Asia, which in Cambodia produced more than three million dead.

We are witnessing these days the death-cry danger of the anti-historical social systems which, confounded by their own crisis, adopt desperate and insane measures. Such is the Chinese alliance with the United States, which moves the world to the brink of a third world war. This alliance, with its all-powerful, boastful hegemonic positions, desires to preserve at any cost a social system already condemned by history. The invasion of Viet Nam by China is no conflict between two socialisms, but rather a criminal attempt to prevent

23

the development of socialism in the Socialist Republic of
Viet Nam. A centrist political party in Mexico, in a public
demonstration, called this clique of Chinese bosses a "secret society of adventurers." And Fidel Castro has called
them a "cabal of habitual delinquents."

Thus imperialism has discovered in China an adequate
and servile instrument for making Southeastern Asia a powder
keg for the third world war.

This unusual situation now forces our present assembly
to protest energetically China's invasion of Viet Nam. We
must affirm our most militant solidarity with the thousand-
fold heroic people of Viet Nam.

It is my privilege to inaugurate this historic International Meeting of Theologians, which assembles Christian
theologians and leaders from Africa, Asia, Europe, both
East and West, the United States and Latin America. We
have chosen an important theme - "Evangelization and Politics" - for our discussion. I can do no less than in the
name of Jesus Christ and as a delegate of the Department of
Theological Studies of the Regional Committee for the Latin
American and Caribbean Christian Peace Conference to announce
that the formal labors of this Meeting have now begun. And
let me state in the name of humanity and of history on this
25th day of February, 1979, in the city of Matanzas, Cuba,
our conviction that "Viet Nam will win!"

*   *   *

WELCOMING ADDRESS

RAUL FERNANDEZ CEBALLOS

It is indeed a double privilege for me, since I welcome you in the name of the Ecumenical Council of Cuba (CEC),consisting of seventeen ecumenical denominations, and in the name of the Latin American and Caribbean Christian Peace Conference.

Cuba rejoices in receiving you in its bosom, so that a beacon can shine from this land of liberty to illuminate the cause which our Christian brothers and sisters should pursue in this crucial hour for humanity.

Cuba opens its arms to offer you a warm welcome, hopeful that these meetings will mark a firm advance in both thought and action throughout the world. We are in the last years of the twentieth century - called the century of enlightenment, when in reality we are living in the densest and darkest obscurity.

A splendid vision appears possible as a fruit of this large meeting of Christian men and women, distinguished for their valuable contributions towards obtaining, once and for all, definite progress towards the shining light promised by Christ.

The message of liberation, peace, justice and full enjoyment of life, with all the rights which human beings deserve, once achieved, will alleviate in great part the tensions which are experienced today.

We Cubans are constantly mindful of our Apostle of Liberty, José Marti, who said, towards the end of the nineteenth century, "It is always the humble, the shoe-less, the homeless, the poor fishermen, who gather shoulder to shoulder to face iniquity and those who release into flight the Gospel with its silvered wings aflame. Truth reveals itself more clearly to the poor and needy."

Marti attended various churches during his exile in the United States. He was a great writer, a fervent orator. In one of his articles, published in La Nación of Buenos Aires, Argentina on May 21, 1887, he wrote in reference to the excommunication of Father M. C. Glyn, "To happiness, Oh you

25

humble! For the Hymn most welcome to God is that of joy for
all God's creatures!" And Marti continued, "As long as one
person is unhappy, someone is to blame." Marti concluded,
"Formerly crusades were organized to redeem the Holy Sepulcher. Today we must organize crusades for peace so that all
of life might not be entombed."

In the issue of La Nación, July 20, 1887, a paragraph
appeared which is of impressive significant for us theologians today, both Cubans and guests. "Since we no longer
wear rawhide garments, since we now read history, since we
have priests and ministers who teach truthful theologies,
since we know that bishops do not come from heaven, since
we know why we have human medias, why then do we have supreme unction? why do we have culpable connections with
princes? why filthy contracts and shameful indulgences,
all made by human hands, all as a simple form of government?"
The concern of Marti is the same as yours, which moved you
to assemble here in this land of Marti's dreams. He urged
that schools be seeded throughout the land so that students
might work the soil while concentrating on their studies of
science and literature.

Another reflection of this teacher. "It is the just
person, educated to work, the laborer, the farmer, the honest
intellectual who, fully aware that s/he is contributing well,
who is interested in the oppressed. This person cooperates
in taking advantage of the benefits of a socialist community.
I say socialist and not capitalist because we have already
experienced the fruits of capitalism; privileges for the few
and misery for the great majority, together with underemploy-
ment, unemployment, illiteracy, malnutrition, premature death
and miserable living conditions."

Marti surmised the character of some bishops in affirming that "Certainly there are some bishops - and I write this
in capital letters to differentiate them from the other bishops - who are defenders of the poor. These will multiply and
become a force."

If Marti were living he would appreciate knowing about
this meeting - and its hope for a world of peace and justice
growing towards the infinite. Yes, it is for this that you
are all receiving our most enthusiastic welcome. You are interested in the diffusion of justice, of peace and in putting
into practice the message of liberation proclaimed by Jesus.

And what is to be said of Latin America and the Caribbean? What can be said about these lovely lands, precious
gift of God, which have been exploited by the few in detriment of the great majority?

How far we are, distinguished brothers and sisters, from
fulfilling the Creator's design!

I refer to the passage in Genesis 1:28-30. "And God
created human beings in God's image, male and female. And
God blessed them, and said, 'Multiply and be fruitful, re-
plenish the earth and enjoy it, have sovereignty over the
fish of the waters, the birds of the air, and all the animals
of the earth.' And God said, 'Here I have given you seeds to
plant so that you might eat. And all the animals of the
land and the birds of the air and the fishes of the sea and
the green plants of the earth shall be for you to eat.' And
so it was."

From this Biblical passage, we learn of our duty to labor, to obtain food, but also the right to exercise sovereignty. And what is sovereignty? Sovereignty is the control
or the command over something, as the owner. It is taking
possession of something, subjecting it to your domination and
management.

History has demonstrated a very different reality. The
true workers of the country and the workers of the city, art-
isans, professionals, producers - all of these have been and
still are living poorly. They labor, but they do not exercise sovereignty. They do not own what they produce. Reflect
for a moment on the slaves of yesterday and the oppressed of
today; then think about those who enrich themselves continuously at the cost of those who in reality are producing,
with their creative labor. Each passing year the rich are
getting richer and the poor, poorer. That imbalance, that
reality cannot please God and it is unjust even in our eyes.

In 1963 during the centennial celebration of the Emancipation Proclamation, Rev. Dr. Martin Luther King, Jr. said,
"In this celebration there was everything to remind the Black
person that s/he was not yet free, that s/he was living in a
veiled slavery, with certain complex adornments."

What can the inhabitants of the so-called Third World
say? All people celebrate their "independence" when, in
reality, the celebration only makes them recall their true
dependence.

You are familiar with vital statistics, especially those of Latin America. The situation has hardly changed since Marti wrote, some ninety years ago. If it has changed, it has become worse. It cannot be God's Will that in many Latin American countries life expectancy is as low as 35 or 40 years while in developed countries it reaches nearly 70 for men and 72 for women. Crimes are committed daily. Thousands die daily through the injustice they suffer. It is not God's Will that "white violence" now kills so many through hunger, disease and subhuman conditions. And what is worse, this lack of concern does not worry many people - not even among Christians. This needs to be emphasized.

Precisely because we are militant Christians we cannot tolerate in today's world such manifest inequality, injustice and inhumanity.

A radical change must be made, favorable to the dispossessed classes, so that the words of Jesus may become real, "I have come that you may have life in abundance." In order to make that 180 degree turnabout we must work hard for unity in producing peace and justice.

The world is divided principally into two forces - the oppressors and the oppressed. Christians are also grouped on one side or the other in economic, social and political matters. They are also divided in their interpretation of the Bible. There is no doubt about that.

The enemies of justice fill their ranks with the very exploited themselves. They are Christian in name and exonerate themselves with very sophisticated arguments.

God utilized the prophets in antiquity. Jesus in His time opted for the oppressed, the poor. Today God uses you, "Society must renew itself. No one can be considered all alone, since every person is a part of the community, of a social class."

Jesus reaffirmed His ministry of liberation when He entered the synagogue and read aloud, "The Spirit of the Lord is upon me. For He has sent me to carry Good News to the poor, to mend the broken hearts and to liberate the captives, to free the oppressed - to preach the year of the Lord." (Luke 4:18-19).

We all agree that whoever is interested in imitating this theology should go to the masses, to the people, to the believers. Problems are going to arise upon popularizing

theological reflections among the people rather than in an
elite class. It will be necessary to direct the theological
torrent and direct it for the benefit of those who truly need
it. A theology is needed which takes us by the hand to evaluate prayer and human conduct in the world today. This theology must look anew at the prophets who come to offer their
lives with the oppressed. The message of liberation proclaimed by Christ must be penetrated. The message of Christ
compels us to discover the richness of Scripture, whose real
meaning has been adulterated. In summary, we need a theology
which makes us conscious that we are co-creators and as such
are waiting for our great contribution so that justice may
shine forever in this world, peace may be resplendent and
love reign among all human beings.

        Brothers and Sisters who have been invited from across
the seas and those from this little island of hospitality, I
conclude by wishing you all the best. May your labors be fruitful, because - to quote Dr. W. Wissert'Hooft, former secretary
of the World Council of Churches - "Relations between Church
and State are entering a new phase. Church-State relations
present a continous problem. It would be vain to hope for a
definitive solution. It parallels the relationship of marriage. Even in the best and most happy of cases it is impossible to resolve all the problems and tensions at once. One
must work unceasingly. If our theologians want to establish
good Church-State relations they will obviously be busy for a
long time." The distinguished theologian is quite right.
You should be very busy and very much worried, because a
great responsibility rests on your shoulders for this world.

        Theologians of liberation have been for some years ex-
pressing themselves on several aspects of the situation,
among them the crisis within the Church itself. They have
been misrepresented by persons of divisive opinions, leading
to a weakening of the true values of the theology of liberation, which is charged with building a better world and with
establishing a true, genuine interpretation of the liberating
message of Jesus Christ.

            *   *   *

WELCOMING ADDRESS

CARLOS MANUEL DE CÉSPEDES

Fr. Manuel welcomed the participants on behalf of the Roman Catholic Church of Cuba.

First, I wish to express our gratitude to the directors of the Evangelical Seminary of Theology in Matanzas for having organized these meetings and for having offered me this opportunity of participating in them.

The chosen theme, "Evangelization and Politics," reminds us immediately of the recent Latin American Bishops Conference held in Puebla, Mexico. They met under the theme, "The Present and Future Evangelization of Latin America" and they also considered the relationship between politics and evangelization. The Final Document of that Conference, Part II, contains a section entitled "Evangelization, Ideologies and Politics." This follows a section concerning "Evangelization, Liberation and Human Promotion." The latter is based on three assumptions which His Holiness John Paul II discussed in his inaugural address, "The Truth about Jesus Christ; the Truth about the Church; the Truth about Man."

"It is truly liberation," he said, "that is developing historically - liberation of people, of the individual and of the various dimensions of existence itself: social, political, economic, educational, cultural in every sense, and their interrelationships. In all of this there circulates the transforming richness of the Gospel, with its specific and appropriate meaning, which we must treasure." (No. 354).

And later he states, "The political dimension, consisting of humankind, represents a facet of human society. It has global dimensions, since its aim is social betterment. But that is not the last word in social relationships. Christian faith does not depreciate political action; on the contrary, it is valued and esteemed highly." (No. 380).

"The Church...feels that it has a duty and a right to enter this arena of reality, since Christianity must evangelize the totality of human existence, including the political." (No. 381).

The Document contains several further references and analyses which justify our confidence that the life of the Church in Latin America will be identified with the Gospel of liberation. Nevertheless I believe that the texts I have cited illustrate sufficiently the position of the pastors of our Church on the subject matter which draws us together at these meetings, which are both theological and ecumenical.

They are ecumenical because we confess different Christian faiths. Ecumenical because of the theological pluralism of the participants. Ecumenical also because of our diverse geographical origins, living our faiths with distinct socio-economic and political and cultural backgrounds.

And so we pledge our entire unaffected and fraternal collaboration in the theological tasks of these days, as Cuban Catholics, trying to bring witness of our Catholic faith - that is, in concert with the Church of Christ Universal. We are walking in hope, animated by charity, knowing that we are in solidarity with our beloved Cuban people, with whom we form a part on this special historic occasion.

We are certain that reflective thought and dialogue - based on our common Christian heritage, faith in our specific confessions and our diverse backgrounds - will enrich the critical discernment which molds our personal and communal viewpoints, towards promoting that which constitutes ultimately the Church's "reason for existence": the living reality of the Gospel of Christ.

*   *   *

EVANGELIZATION AND POLITICS

FROM THE CUBAN POINT OF VIEW

SERGIO ARCE MARTINEZ

Introduction

Allow me to take advantage of being one of the representatives of Cuba, the country wherein this meeting is taking
place; of being the rector of the Evangelical Seminary of
Theology of Matanzas, one of the host institutions of the
event, and, in particular, the place where it is being held;
and, finally, of being vice president of the Latin American
and Caribbean Christian Peace Conference, thereby sharing
with the Secretary General and other vice presidents the
broadest representation of our world-wide movement in this
meeting. Thus I feel obliged to try to summarize some of
the basic generalities by which we would like to see our
dialogue oriented.

We speak from our perspective as Cuban Christians, a
perspective determined in great part by the experience we
have shared with our people throughout these years of struggle. First, our perspective has been shaped by the triumph
and then by the consolidation of our socialist revolution,
which now in 1979 is celebrating its twentieth anniversary.

This revolutionary experience, so rich and pregnant with
accomplishments that speak eloquently for the justification
of its existence, has benefited the Cuban Church significant-
ly. This experience in turn has obliged us morally to organize and work for these meetings, with the help of many comrades, colleagues and friends.

Our only objective in organizing and working for this
event has been to create an appropriate framework for seeking
and finding a common denominator for mobilizing ourselves.
We need a common understanding of our theological task which
comes as the product of a serious commitment to society in
its struggle for liberation. We can reflect on this task
here through discussions among ourselves which are open,

fraternal and sincere.

The obsession - if that is what you wish to call it - of the Cuban revolution for obtaining unity in the anti-imperialist struggle, in the search for a peace based upon just relations between nations, and in diminishing the tyrannies of nations which impede the popular movements for liberation, is a lesson which we have tried to learn. What interests us most in this case is unity. It should not be a unity which is placed above us nor in opposition to really fundamental issues, but rather a unity founded on principles which are clear, concrete and defined by experience in struggle. This much we have managed to learn - if not everything - especially those of us who have dedicated ourselves to theological tasks in socialist Cuba.

We do not believe that the acheivement of unity is an easy objective for Christians to attain, particularly for those dedicated specifically to theological tasks. The sectarian spirit which moves us all at times and the theological error of confusing practical theology with revelation may be, and occasionally has been, an impregnable stockade. We are given to thinking that our words - eminently human, and at times inhuman - are the words of God.

Theology is a human occupation. "All that has been said about God" - says one pinnacle of theology - "has been said by human beings." Therefore we theologians should be the most humble of intellectuals - after all, we are discussing things about which we are ignorant; this makes us at times the most vain and overly proud of eminent geniuses of pedantry.

Very serious problems for conducting a truly fruitful dialogue arise from such pride and lack of humility, such vanity and pedantry. Exaggerated hautiness does not lead to dialogue.

This dialogue now should seek unity, perhaps like that once proposed by Enrique Dussel. He suggested that we seek an "international division of theological labor." While we believe in a unity based on principles which are defined, clear and concrete, we also maintain that the dialogue and the unity which we seek cannot extend beyond certain basic premises of agreement.

The first of these premises I shall describe in negative terms. The unity of legitimate contemporary theological occupation cannot be sought in an explanation embracing the totality of the theological universe. Theories which explicitly express the theological universe in a more or less rational foundation do not build unity.

At this level if we emphasize and dangerously overvalue such a form of theological occupation, we could not speak of "the point of contact" which propitiates the enriching, creative and laboriously constructed dialogue.

The Gospels and the social, political and economic realities of today make this meeting urgent.

With realistic judgment we are soon to learn that through that route we do not find any common ground sufficiently generalized to be accepted. Nor is it sufficiently specific in its elaboration to be able to serve us as an adequate foundation. We cannot hope for quite one hundred percent agreement in method. If we seek complete agreement we shall frequently find ourselves bound by prefabricated conventions which mean little or nothing.

I recall that someone left the theological meetings in Mexico in 1977 calling me nothing less than "Stalinist." In this way we enter into trench warfare, but what does that matter in a world living amidst apocalyptic signs where war, hunger and death - all products of imperialist exploitation - are struggling to commence the final moribund conflict against peace, society and the life of a new world? To do this would be a fine intellectual exercise. Such verbal warfare would perhaps be agreeable enough aesthetically but it would only be a spiritual jeer.

On this road we would soon be situated - or others would place us - under certain protective patron saints whom we would not be able to change, unless we initiated an open and frank dialogue - which, however, is always productive. This situation would change only if, by a miracle, a praxis were to be committed, devoted to the masses.

If this last point were not the purpose of every one of you who has accepted our invitation to be integrated into this conference, then there would be, at least for me, a tremendous frustration. Who could be certain that, like the Pharisee of the Parable, there might not be in our midst that one who prays for us like the Pharisee, "Lord, I thank you that I am not like other men, particularly like that Publican"? If that were so we could gain little or nothing from all the initiative, time and energy which we have invested in organizing this event.

The road to be followed must not be structured rigidly, but sufficiently clearly so that those of us who are trying to activate the teachings of Jesus as a revoluationary force and to stimulate evangelization as a political, anti-imperialist and anti-capitalist activity can be lead to the task with a sound understanding. Then, if anyone has already lubricated his/her intellectual machine gun and is preparing a rhetorical arsenal for shattering the icon of the "theology" of an old antagonist of a supposed new antagonist, then we must ask this person to calm his/her spirits. We must make a strong attack against but one fortress: that which houses the enemies of unity. We must seek a constructive dialogue and aim for the conversion of all so that we can become the "voice of the voiceless."

This is not to say that we should not challenge our ideas. What I would like to say is that "if we bite ourselves and chew ourselves, we must watch out lest we destroy ourselves." Such self destruction would not benefit the "poor" of the world, nor would it benefit the cause of the Kingdom of God. And, at least here in Cuba, we are held in admiration and watched carefully by those who look to the Church.

Those of us who have planned this meeting, did not do so hoping to organize a boxing match, as in New York or in Chicago. We did not give so much love, care and sacrifice for this. If we were interested in boxing - as it is good at time to be - we would at least have a socialist order in this bout. That is we would not only have technical regulations, but we would also have provisions for protection against injuries!

The second premise is that the dialogue and the unity for which we strive is possible. "Peace," said the Psalmist, "is possible." The Psalmist was thinking of the peace which "embraces justice" and which in Biblical language is included in the struggle for "that truth which is humiliated by injustice." This is possible when our theological activities are conceived, primarily, less as transformations in the conceptualization of the universal theology than as the political reality which fundamentally determines evangelization.

At that level of confrontation we will find the possible point of contact which, being sufficiently generalized in its acceptance and specific in its practical particularity, makes

our task possible. Or, is it that I am too optimistic or in-
genuous in thinking that all who are here today are dedicated
to the truth: the truth which is the commitment to the practice of Biblical justice, which is distributive practice? The
social-economic contexts of any one of us might be either
partially or wholly different, but even so, might they not
lead us to a concrete historical and political concept of
the significance of the Gospels for the world of today?

Finally, a third premise. The unity we are discussing
is not uniformity. The exhausting search for truth signifies
a struggle for justice, not in proto-historic nor meta-his-
toric terms, but in intra-historic terms. This means that
our struggle for justice cannot - in terms of a Kingdom which
lost itself or a Kingdom which will betray us - violate ideal-
istically the concrete process which makes it real and true,
according to the laws of social development. Rather, it con-
tributes concretely to the process or processes which make it
possible, in conformity with the same dialectic of history.

Dialectics, said Lenin, has to do with connections, with
relationships, and not with isolated things considered one
after another. Dialectics in our situation should have to do
with the connections and relationships which we discover among
ourselves, in order to deepen them. These relationships exist
in our common theological tasks not primarily in the school
of the "current" or the "particular" theology to which each
of us belongs, ignoring or disdaining all others. Dialectics
in our work lies truly in the connections and relations which
we are able to describe and emphasize between our different
theological fields and activities as far as they are "true"
connections and relations. If they are true connections and
relations they will serve in the concrete establishment of
the "love of justice" in this world.

Evangelization: Crux of the Church

The Church is evangelical or it is not the Church of Jesus Christ. Wherever it evangelizes, and only there, is it
the Church. The"signs" of the Church consist of one "sign"
alone: evangelization. The so-called "signs" are evangelical
or they are not "signs" of the presence of the Church, which
is the "presence of Christ."

The "means of grace" of the Church are reduced to one

"means:" evangelization. The so-called "means of grace" are
evangelical or they are not "means of grace" as a gift of the
Holy Spirit. To be an evangelical is to have a militant commitment throughout one's life and death to Jesus Christ and
His teaching, that is to say, to His Kingdom.

The teaching, which is in itself an event, is conceived
of Biblically as the "good news for the poor." In that sense
and only thus, it is converted into "good news" for all humankind. The historic subject of Christ's teachings, as an
event, is the "rich man who made himself poor, for us, so
that we might be enriched through His poverty." In this
lies grace, according to the same Pauline text. Poverty here
refers not only to the Franciscan discipline of possessing
nothing; but more importantly it refers to not being possessed by anything but Jesus Christ, the poor person par excellence. The question posed by the Apostle Peter to Jesus re-
garding which of them possesses nothing except Jesus, through
not being possessed by any thing but Jesus gives us a clue
to the situation about which we are speaking.

Evangelization is a "double event," an unforseen happening on two fronts. On one hand it concerns the "repro-
duction" of the event of Jesus' teaching. And on the other
it is the human re-action to the divine action which takes
concrete form historically in the "liberation from all oppression." The historical subjects of the evangelization are
the poor, the oppressed, the dispossessed.

Evangelization as action is intimately inter-related with
the subject which determines it. This subject is historical
and therefore materializes itself in the event. All claims
that evangelizing action depends on idealizing the historic
subject are inverted and false. This is of extreme importance
when one wants to understand the meaning of evangelization
for every historic moment, in any place.

What has been said does not deny that there are some
fundamental questions which characterize the subject, at
least from the viewpoint of the evangelizing event. The subject evangelizes "with no purse, no robe nor sandals." The
fact of his/her poverty opens the doors of the "Kingdom
which is coming." Those who are dedicated to the imminence
of the Kingdom, no others - and many claim it - are the true
evangelists. If the rich pretend to be dedicated, the result
is an absurdity, an unreality, a stupidity, and what is worse,

a demonic invention. Evangelization becomes "opium of the poor."

Evangelization, re-action of the poor committed to the "good news from the Poor," signifies the event of the evangelist reproduced by the poor who assume as their own the "good news" of the imminent and urgent coming of the Kingdom. We speak here of the poor who have ceased being the sort of poor who aspire to be rich in a publican sense, that is, in individualistic terms, egotistically. We are not speaking here of that which is unspiritual or immoral. The unspiritual is the truly materialistic, just as the immoral is the truly anti-human.

"Publicanism" is the grave sin of the Church and of many Christians. "Publicanism" is the negation of the Gospels because anyone can "proselytize," but only those who are living evangelists can evangelize. Only those who have "consciousness" of their own poverty in contrast with the riches of the rich can truly evangelize; but they must not aspire individually to overcome poverty and make themselves newly rich following the well beaten path of exploitation, oppression and lies, which is injustice. They must not be individualists, denying that the Gospels also portray the death and historical disappearance of Christ.

There are also "the poor of Yahweh." These poor do not have the "consciousness of the poor" in contrast with the rich. Rather, they are the poor in the service of "poverty." In the genuine evangelization of the poor, as the subject of the re-action corresponding to the evangelical event, they do not act only as the poor, conscious of their poverty in contrast with the rich; but rather they act as the poor conscious that their poverty is at the service of other poor people. This is the poverty of zealots, not the poverty of publicans.

The historical subject of the Gospels portrays that which was announced in the characterization of His soul as the subject whose "arm intervenes with strength, undoing the plans of the self-loving, overthrowing the throne of the powerful and exalting the humble, filling the hungry with good things and sending the rich away empty." This despoiling of the rich determines the genuineness of the subject. On the other hand the Gospels - "the good news for the poor" - are the Gospels of the Kingdom. The Kingdom belongs to the poor

and "is at their gates." Any lesson or doctrine on the Kingdom which does not strictly consider the intimate relation
between its nearness and its inheritors or possessors disturbs
the meaning of the Gospels, as preached by Jesus. The dialectic of the Gospels on the Kingdom affirms that the poor person
is the rich person who became poor in order that through this
poverty we might become enriched.

When in the Old Testament riches are considered as a sign
of divine blessing, this is not to be scorned. Neither should
we be confused when it speaks of the poor as the chosen of
Yahweh. Neither riches nor poverty in and of themselves and
for the sake of themselves is the question here.

The Gospels make all values relative which human beings
feel themselves tempted to make absolute. The history of Genesis 3 is the history of the absolutization of the relative
values of "good" and "bad." The road which leads to riches
or to poverty is the one which has value for the Gospel of
"the Way." It is the case of Job, who finally becomes richer
than he was previously because of his experiences of poverty.
In the dialectics of the Gospels the Kingdom belongs to the
rich who were or who made themselves poor. The road to riches is poverty at the service of the poor.

As long as the Church remains rich through taking the
road of the unredeemed rich, to foment its riches, this Church
will not be able to evangelize. It is impossible to speak of
evangelizing in a continent of poor people such as Latin America unless the relationship between the Church and the rich
is clarified. A basic principle making this clarification
must be established and followed.

Politics: The Crux of Evangelization

All that we have said until now can be said by many.
Jesus Christ said it and Judas Iscariot affirmed it, even
correcting the Master, whom he accused of being a traitor
to the cause of the poor. We read about this option for
the poor in the final working papers from the meetings held
in Oaxtepec and Puebla. The Pope speaks of serving the poor
and so does Jimmy Carter in his Sunday School classes. President Carter has even spoken about it in his public addresses.
Camilo Torres and Nestor Paz preached it, as have the new
"evangelists" who swarm over Latin America and the Third
World, financed by the great trans-nationals.

It is implicit in the publications of the Trilateral
Commission and the speeches of Fidel; in the proclamations of
the leaders of heroic Viet Nam and in those of the traitors
who today are usurping power in China.

Herein lies the relevancy, whether we like it or not,
whether we recognize it or not, of politics. Politics are
the "fruit" of the tree. "By their fruits shall you know
them. It is not enough to go around saying 'Lord, Lord' to
enter the Kingdom of Heaven. One must put to work the plan of
our Heavenly Creator. On that day many will say 'Lord! Lord!
Yes, we have prophesied in your name.' And then I shall de-
clare to them, 'I have never known you. Be gone from me,
you who practice wickedness.'"

"All who hear these my words, and put them to work, are
like the wise person who built a house upon a rock. The rains
came, the flood rose, the gales blew, and they beset the
house, but it did not fall, since it lay firm upon the rock.
And all who hear these my words and do not put them to work
will appear like the foolish one who built a house on sand.
The rains fell, the flood rose, the winds blew, they set
upon the house and it fell. And great was the fall!"

In May of 1944 Bonhoeffer wrote about the generation
which would succeed his own. He said, "You will manifest
a new relationship between thought and action. You will
think only of whatever will be responsible for your action.
For us, our thinking was often only the luxury of being a
spectator; for you, thinking will be totally at the service
of action."

We speak often - and in general we speak well - of a theology which starts out with praxis and goes on to reflection.
Still, to develop this methodological premise - however valid
and renewing - into a dogma, makes it counterproductive and
unreal. This would not be consistent with the concrete reality of the task of theology as it presents itself today. To
set it up as the center for discussion would be, in my humble
understanding, almost Byzantine. It, in fact, resembles the
Byzantine riddle my Grandmother used to ask me as a child, to
confuse me, "Which comes first: the egg or the hen?"

The problem is encountered, from our perspective and
context, on all sides. It is said that the first word of
theology is committed action, that reflection must be secondary. I have no doubt that this is so in many cases.

41

In reference to this question, I am reminded of a discussion a few months ago during the Student Christian Movement Conference held in Caracas, Venezuela. There I said, "I have no objection to this if 'primary' and 'secondary' refer to rank and not to chronological sequence. The question is trivial and innocuous in that it is theoretically and abstractly insoluble. Which is primary, the egg or the hen? What is important here is not which one came first in time. What is truly important is the interaction of theory and practice in producing theological activity - in the specific situation of a people being oppressed because of its struggle for liberation." I then continued with a quote from Lenin and ended by saying, "What is important is that theological reflection, or theory (the matter we tried to consider in the preceeding section) and political action (what we are describing in this section) should generate and affect one another mutually; should be controlled mutually; and are mutually verified."

At that meeting I spoke before Latin Americans. Now I am addressing a more international audience, but I make the same affirmation. The problem of the egg and the hen is insoluble theoretically. In a specific situation and time, the question might be answered. In the abstract such an answer is impossible, without making tactical and strategic mistakes, since the answer must depend on what is at hand - the egg, or the hen. Ultimately it is a problem, if you will, of economics, as are all historical problems. An egg may be bought for a few cents, but not a hen. If I have enough to buy a hen, the first priority for me then would be the hen. But having a hen would not mean that I could dogmatically proclaim its universal priority over the egg. Nor could I proclaim universal priority for hens if I owned a chicken farm. I would have no greater right to generalize universally than if I had their output of eggs - or a single egg.

In Latin America and the rest of the underdeveloped world and in a Church such as ours in the so-called Third World, we have to start with the egg of praxis. Throughout the centuries of "Christian" civilization, of uncompassionate exploitation, of obscure oppression and many sided dependence, we have not counted on the resources which might make a different course possible. As poor orphans of all wealth, we

possess nothing but political action, the promise of liberation, the egg, the originator of creative action. Under
these circumstances our raison d'etre is the preeminence of
praxis. This we see as the only recourse for the poor,
those for "whom is the Kingdom." Nevertheless to deny for
this reason other peoples' right, which they have, to protect and defend the hen of reflective thought - even though
it be a luxury, in the best meaning of the word, of the privileged, of the rich, of the oppressor - to deny them all
rights of theological reflection beyond what they have and
what they are appears to me to be taking us too far. We ourselves have benefited from and we continue to profit from all
that in our "second" moment, not to speak of the "first."
We shall be able to compel them to give their wealth to those
who have none in order that we may all take advantage of the
wealth which has accumulated for them alone. But to reject
the hen, throw it away deplumed to be devoured by the wolves
for fattening themselves still more, appears to me absurd both
tactically and strategically. It seems to me better that we
share and thus enrich our boneyard of common starvation.

What does matter, in this case as in others, as Bonhoeffer adds, is that we have only to "think of that which we
shall have to do to make ourselves responsible for our action.
It is not a question of the 'right' of the thinker, but of
the 'duty' of the doer."

The theological thinker has no right - especially in comparison with any other thinker - to be merely a spectator.
This would be most inacceptable, particularly in this age.
One must renounce being a mere spectator, - even if in the
first row. The thinker must be primarily at the service of
action. What is needed is that theologcial reflection or
thinking and political action should generate and stimulate
one another mutually, should be mutually controlled and mutually verified.

One might deduce from these heights of our dissertation
that evangelization is not theological reflection, properly
speaking. Nevertheless, the "kerygma" - proclamation - as represented in the New Testament is theological reflection of
the Church. To conclude the critique on that sermon, the
author of the Book of Acts states, "Those who accepted His
words did baptise themselves and some day they shall benefit
three thousand fold."

"They were constant in attending the teaching of the apostles, in the community of life, in sharing food and in prayer. The multitude was impressed by the many miracles and cures which the apostles performed." From this we might hope for descriptions of the "miracles" and "cures," but the author then says, "The believers lived all together and owned every-thing in common; they sold their goods and possessions and divided the proceeds according to the needs of each one."

Evidently politics is represented here as the area which designates decisively the evangelistic significance of the kerygma, in so far as evangelization converts itself into praxis as a consequence of loving justice. The central mes-sage of Acts is that without political action, evangelization has no real meaning, no real validity. Without political action, evangelization is nothing more "than sounding brass or tinkling cymbals." Must we recapitulate the history of Western Christianity to argue that statement?

Political praxis has always mediated evangelization and de-evangelization. Nevertheless there is the other danger - that of making politics absolute. The Gospels are not poli-tics. The evangelizing mediation of the kerygma is impreg-nated by politics. There are many profound citations on this subject from representatives of a variety of different theo-logical schools and traditions, including Bultmann. However, this is not the place to cite them.

If the Gospels were politics, we would have to consider the politics of Jesus as absolute. From this I conclude that those who consider Jesus as non-political are as much in error as those who in recent times present Him as political. The danger of exaggerating every discovery of any aspect of truth is ever with us. The former, of the non-political Jesus, wish or try to make us think that they are speaking of Jesus. Nev-ertheless, the false depolitization of Jesus is really trying to hide from us an evangelization which is false in being un-political. Once evangelization assumes the political medium, we find ourselves committing ourselves with the poor to the struggle for the establishment of a peace which embraces jus-tice. The love for justice in this world becomes important.

The latter, those of the political Jesus, endeavoring to defend their position, often present us with the politics of Jesus as being the determiner for the political mediation of the Gospels, in all places and times.

Jesus was political first, because all His actions and teachings had a political color. Jesus was not only a doctrine. Jesus was also an evangelist. He mediated His teachings – which were found within Himself – politically. Otherwise He would not have been crucified, and much less, between two guerrillas. Some of those who present Jesus as political are actually de-politicizing the Christian of today and the present evangelization of the Church. This is one of the contradicitions and paradoxes facing us.

Jesus praised the Good Samaritan and condemned the priest and the Levite. This does not mean, however, that our political actions are limited to this. Today the correlation of forces is such that the peoples' struggles for liberation are being favored. The "Hebrews" who lie wounded and dying on the highways of the world are rising up to exterminate the robber, imperialism.

Jesus did not join the Zealots against the Roman Empire or rebel openly against the establishment in Gethsemane. This does not mean, however, that Camilo Torres took an anti-evangelical path. It does not mean that he was not involved in evangelization. This does not mean that our long list of Christian martyrs for the cause of liberation in Latin America during the past decade is inconsistent with the Gospel. It is not a condemnation of their method for evangelization. For truly the most genuine Christian model of the century is not Albert Schweitzer; but rather, it is Camilo Torres.

Jesus was a poor person who had a "consciousness of poverty in the service of the poor." He condemned the rich to remain outside of the Kingdom, inviting them to voluntarily give up their riches. Jesus laid aside an analysis of the mechanisms which were producing these human miseries. This does not mean, however, that today we should not employ Marxist analyses of society's development in order to understand the reason why there are both rich and poor in the world. In so doing, we do not deny the Gospel nor our task of evangelization among the masses.

Jesus fed the multitude by multiplying the loaves and fishes. He did not formulate or subscribe to a theory of revolution involving the giving of "our daily bread." This does not mean that we should not subscribe to the revolutionary theory which has proven to be the only effective one for changing the unjust social, economic and political

structures that are causing hunger, illness and misery. This
does not prevent us from installing more equitable structures
which permit lives of dignity for all. I am saying here, that
this position of Jesus does not prevent us from subscribing to
Marxism-Leninism in theory and practice.

No objective student of the Bible can deny the political
activity of Jesus. The evidence of His option for the poor
is definitive. Still, the meaing of "poor" during His lifetime and today, because of the objective differences in political, economic and social development between the two per-
iods, cannot be compared. The realistic political implementation of an option for the poor by Jesus cannot be compared
at all with that which we in the twentieth century can create.
This explains why, occasionally, an anarchist feels closer to
Jesus than a socialist does. But it also explains why there
are so many efforts to conciliate Marxist socialist theory.
It helps us understand why there are so many efforts to scorn
certain theoretical aspects of Marx which inconvenience us.
This distance between two stages of society's development
also helps us understand why some people today even attempt
to deny Lenin and his revolution with all its historical significance. Thus a Bishop who attended the Conference in
Puebla made headlines when he said, "Socialism, yes; but not
as in Cuba!"

The picture of a socially inadaptable Jesus, lacking solutions to the political, economic and social problems of His
people, can cause great confusion when we accept such a picture and use it in the present political, economic and social
situation. If we really wish to be Christians, we must dis-
tinguish between the Gospels and the process for their mediation - evangelization.

What does a Gospel of "Good News for the poor" mean today to subjects who are poor? For us in Cuba this has been
an excruciating question for twenty years. Who is, or are,
the historic subjects of evangelization? Who are the poor
today? Who are the poor in the United States, in Europe, in
underdeveloped countries? in Cuba? in Viet Nam?

The system of production in Jesus' land and time, with a
low level of development, witnessed a universal poverty which
cannot be compared with the diversity and specialization which
present day capitalism has produced - a system now in its imperialist maturity. How can one insert into this obvious

situation the fact that socialist countries shine on every
continent, freed from the chains of imperialist oppression?
How can one explain the fact that the Pope's address in Puebla was received by Pinochet with approval and by a Mexican
Indian with enthusiasm? How do we explain the Chinese invasion of Viet Nam? How can we understand a Cuba which
supports the struggles for liberation in Africa? Who, then,
are the poor, the historical subjects of liberation?

I shall not answer the question exhaustively. I shall
only indicate a path towards clarification. Can we continue
talking about the poor today, on a global scale, as historical
subjects of evangelization? Most certainly we can, always,
whenever we are cognizant that they are the ones who in this
capitalist world have resisted the pressures and the repression which force them to conceive of their poverty not only
as the opposite of wealth, but also as the only means for
enriching the poor. It is a matter of poor people in the process of acquiring class consciousness. This new element of
class is included here. Class is so evident in the development of capitalism. Classes have been necessary and have
been used to determine the development of capitalism in
accordance with the development of productive forces in
certain areas and sub-areas of today's world. Classes have
been used to "globalize" the sense of poverty under which
we suffer today.

Today we must ask,"How many theologians are considering
the class struggle as an essential element of analysis in
their work? How many are taking it seriously?" But in order
to take it seriously, it is also essential to consider most
attentively the triumph of the working class in many areas
and sub-areas of the world. This shows the working class to
be the revolutionary class not only in theory, but also in
practice.

At the same time the new situations which create themselves and present themselves demand our constant alertness.
We must always maintain receptivity and disposition to any
new realistic political mediation which is appropriate.

If the Church and its theologians desire to stop apply-
ing brakes to social development and to always ride - with a
push - in the caboose of the train of history, they must of
necessity consider all aspects of every new situation.

Finally, the high level of technology developed by capitalist productivity has complicated the situation greatly. Capitalist development always produces as a by-product the underdevelopment of vast numbers of human beings, of nations and entire continents. Recognition of this fact leads us anew to reconsider the poor as the historic subjects of evangelization and, therefore, of political mediation at the present moment of world history.

In our case in Cuba the solution of this problem for the Church and its theologians is unavoidably urgent. The relationship between evangelization and politics - the role of the poor as subjects in the making of history giving witness to the Word - is indeed the Achilles heal of today's Church. It is the challenge facing the Churh's task of evangelization and theological labor, its efficacy and efficiency.

Evangelization and Politics: Their Mutual Genesis

Evangelization and politics generate one another mutually. There is no pre-established, dogmatic priority of either over the other. Still there is no doubt that if we had received a Gospel void of politics, politics would have quickly imposed itself. In the final verses of Acts 2 we see clearly how one thing after another was generated mutually in the primitive Church. They are inter-mixed with each other in a generative, creative sequence. Hence, it appears that the appropriate task of theology is to mediate the cultural revolution of the world today to those Christians who denegrate it. This mediation should be to expiate or conciliate a "conversion" of the Church, a conversion to history. Once the Church experiences this conversion, it will indeed be a true conversion to God. For several centuries now, with the advent of modernism, the Church has turned its back to history. This is the other factor which makes it appear as if politics had priority in the process of evangelization.

Nevertheless it is impossible to make an evangelical judgment of politics if the latter in turn is not generated by a minimal remnant of legitimately Christian kerygma, hidden inside of the false evangelization. Herein lies the power of the Gospels, the dynamo of the Word of God and our only "hope against hope," which in turn drives on our poor theological faculties and our battered pastoral responsibility.

Nevertheless, this remnant is revealed to us as soon as we enter the arena of politics. Unless the Church recognizes the politics of mediation within the Scriptures, the Church will remain relegated to the roadside of our triumphant socialist revolution. Unless the Church recognizes that, according to the Scriptures themselves, politics is involved in the mediation of the Gospel, the Church will miss the historical moment for participation in the construction of a new society and in the creation of the new human being.

I do not need to explain that today the political arena generated by the kerygma —while at the same time mutually generating the evangelizing kerygma - is the social liberation which the construction of socialism represents. To explain this would carry us into other themes, which are not specifically in order for this presentation.

I understand that very few in this hall doubt that today Marxism gives us the scientific key which facilitates integration of true liberation of the individual with ecclesiastic and social liberation. Marxism explains and provides us with theoretical and practical instruments, so that social liberation becomes integrated with one and all of us as individuals, making us persons, together with liberating the Church so that it can really evangelize.

People are not stones, neither are they lapdogs fed with enriched food to make them sparkle and glow - so that they serve to feed the aesthetic pride of their owners. Mothers may try to fatten their children with vitamins to make them sleek and proud, winning prizes in child-rearing. But these children are no more human than those of normal weight.

Poor children in developed capitalist countries and the vast masses of poor in underdeveloped countries live in grime, rarely reaching normal anatomical, physiological nor mental levels. This has cogent meaning for human liberation. The problem is no longer one of the individual; it is a social problem requiring social liberation. It is a problem that requires liberation from structured, built-in economic and political oppression. It requires liberation from a worldwide system which condemns seventy percent of humankind to die of hunger, sickness and malnutrition. And worse, this system takes for granted the moral validity of the exploitation of the majority by a privileged minority. This antihuman situation demands a liberating action, not only for individuals but for all of society. Unless all of society is liberated, there will be no liberation.

All of this carries two fundamental implications. First, there is no such thing as liberation of a single person all alone, which merits being called liberation. It simply does not exist. Either we are all liberated or no one is liberated. Second, that the individual is never self-liberated, all alone. There are no spiritual resources within a single person all alone; no possibility of liberation, in the integral and Christian sense, within an individual. Thus the need for a redeemer or liberator, the necessity for a Christ. The true hero is not the "rare bird," the extraneous entity. The heroic is not in being singular. What happens is that, because of its rarity in a world which prizes singularity, the individual hero might appear to be one who affirms, when in reality it is one who denies himself/herself.

This has been the mistake of more than one Christian, of more than one Church. Furthermore, we should say in addition that it is the sin of all classical theology - especially of Protestants, who are essentially from the bourgeoisie. It is an error into which we all fall, at some time, in one way or another, under the influence of a culture whose rampant and unhealthy individualism has sought to curb more than one attempt at reform or renewal in modern and contemporary times.

Given the stage of the revolution we are in, we must openly confront this individualism which harbors or even nurtures counter-revolution. We must use our revolutionary experience from wherever we are inserted whether it be quietly or stridently, on the margin or in the middle. Some of us may find that we have conditioned our incorporation into the revolutionary process with pretensions of individualisms.

We have had and we still have some Christians who lament that we have not been able to reclaim, wash, rinse and dry the filthy and decalcified bones of our illustrious dead, the skeletons of our ideological corpses which we exhibited superstitiously in the past. We have had, and we still have, Christians who lament that we have been unable to delight our children with the unnecessary luxuries which abounded in the past for the privileged classes. Naturally, what we had then was a dead skeleton, most unsavory, but we escaped its offensive odor with quantities of solemn incense, to avoid nauseating ourselves. The children we cultured, delightful

and overnourished, should be the same as those cultured by
the Pleides of the great "lovers of the yellow king of the
people." The least that should have happened to them was to
die. We knew not how to sing while crying, nor to cry sing-
ing with the poet, "All the more if you think you love the
yellow king of the people. Die with me? Live impure? You
are not alive, my son!"

We did not think, and some do not think even today, that
"God is not the God of the dead, but of the living." Yahweh
is the God who is revealed in the liberation of the oppressed,
the God who commands us not to limit God to a graven image
made during a certain stage of historical development, however sophisticated it might be. In order for us to know
this God of the living, we must "do justice, walk righteously
and defend the cause of the poor and the oppressed." This
God was born in a manger, as life ever renewed. And yes,
this God died on the cross, yet "death no longer masters
Him."

The aesthetic state of existence to which Kierkegaard
referred was the existence of singular individuality, or individualistic singularity, "of which pleasure is the essence."
The automatic enjoyments of cloistered monks, sectarian auto-
complacency, or the automatic satisfaction of the restricted
ghetto are parts of this aesthetic state. The bourgeois
personality - which beyond doubt we have helped create - is one
who lives in this aesthetic state. It is enough to analyze
the historic process of bourgeois capitalism as a political,
economic and social system, which has voided contemporary
imperialism, to make us note this truth, wherein all - exploited and exploiters alike - make themselves victims of the system, in one way or another, its slaves.

The reason is obvious. The liberation of a single person alone is that of a mutilated subhuman, a proto-person,
and the Christ of this liberation would be a theological
monster. This Christ would have no spirit. This Christ
would not have been properly incarnated at birth, but na-
turalized, animalized. Human liberation which pretends to
restrict itself to individual liberation, taking it as a
standard or measure, is mutilating the person, lowering the
definition of humanity. It is a form of becoming one with
the beasts; it is a blasphemy to Christ. This individual
approach to liberation is a denial of the incarnation. It

is to say, "He did not come in the flesh." This would be the
liberation of the "beast," whose liberation returns it to the
jungle anew, in a vicious cycle beyond salvation. It cannot
be said to concern a purely "spiritual" liberation because
that would be to return to repeating what we have done already,
to our shame. By reducing liberation to the individual, we
raising the jungle to the status of heaven, making God a veg-
etable peddler or a capitalist manager. Or in the best of
cases, God becomes a fascist dictator.

On the other hand, the liberty of the Church is not mea-
sured, as any other so-called bourgois liberty, by patron
saints who are outside of the evangelical norms of liberty.
The Church is fundamentally free when it sees itself unim-
peded by forces outside of itself. It is free when it can
uninterruptedly follow the Word of God and be obedient to
Christ, the liberator.

Ecclesiastic liberation will be what concerns us as
Christians specifically, taking into account our identity
in the world as religious professionals.

The Church springs forth from Christianity to the degree
that Christianity is a religion. The Christian is a person
with something unique, peculiar, that which is called faith.
Faith is a most peculiar phenomenon, essentially subjective.
It is, in fact, the supreme subjectivism. Genuine religiosity
is to "know oneself as such," that is, as a subject. This
one must do subjectively, without any objective mediation, in
a direct confrontation with the subject - with no objectivity
possible. That is to say, one must know oneself with God.
It is an absolute self-awareness which, for this reason, is
an instantaneous hetero-acknowledgement. It is an understanding which has no formal methodology for mediation whatsoever. It is an understanding acquired with neither measurement nor temporal bounds. It is the "ray of light" which illuminated Paul on the road to Damascus, "the voice which was
heard," the "invisible light," "the silent voice." Faith
has no mediation, nor any content. It is the eternal, the
unconditional, the "other," which takes us outside of all
time and contingency, outside of our here and now, removing
us from our egocentrism and making us exist for others,
"to live for our neighbors."

Faith properly speaking does not teach; it does not in-
struct. That which teaches and instructs is hope. Faith
does not communicate. That which communicates is love of
action and hope for reasonableness. Che Guevara said to

Fidel, "The faith you impress us with." Faith is passed on, it reflects itself, it imprints itself. With its impact it transforms us to feeling, seeing, hearing "things indescribable, which no human eye has seen." Faith is a bulwark of singularity which does not particularize its universalisms. From this comes "the madness of faith," its somersaults, its scandals. The human being is a universal which does not tolerate particularization, but quite to the contrary. No person is an angel. No one is God. A person is less, "a little below God" – but not God.

The religious status of human existence, said Kierkegaard, is the supreme subjectivity, and "its essence is suffering." When the exiled Spanish poet Leon Felipe argued with the eternal, he claimed that he –the poet – shed "the tear." Jesus admits no alternative from religiosity in His parable of the publican and the Pharisee. The only adoration possible – the only religiosity acceptable to the Creator – is that of, "Sinner, atonement through me." The other religiosity is the Pharisee's, that "He will never be justified." This is related to what Paul said, "God clothed us in disobedience in order to have compassion on us all."

Ecclesiastic liberation, the liberation of religious people, will have to relate to liberation from "sin," and everything "which is not faith is sin." It is a liberation of everything which is not faith. Nevertheless let us be clear. "The just person will be justified by faith." The unjust is not justified. That would be a contradiction in terms. When Paul speaks of justification of the "unjust" he is speaking in a different context. Otherwise it would be a blasphemy and a deceit. Faith does not justify injustice. The unjust – and their injustices – have no justification at all. Whatever is unjust in us has no justification. It is not properly of faith; it is not religious. That which is admittedly "being religious" is justice, not injustice. Injustice relegates itself; it is not "relegated." Injustice is not faith, but it is sin. The unjust person who pretends to be justified by faith is the intellectual person of whom Paul speaks. Paul knows very well what he is doing when in Corinthians 1:3, speaking of the "knowledge of God," of having the mentality of Christ, he contrasts the spiritual person not with the carnal but with the intellectual. The intellectual justifies his/her injustices. S/he is the Phari-

53

see. This is what James describes ironically in his Epistle, certainly not in contradiction to Paul, but quite the contrary, "Show me your faith without works that I will show you my faith for works." James concludes, "Faith without works is dead." Paul supports this without a doubt, although Luther does not.

Ecclesiastic liberation consists of liberating faith from the intellectual interpretation of the Pharisee. We must liberate the Church from the hands of the Pharisees. Like the Christians of the Middle Ages, or lika Unamuno at the tomb of Don Quixote, we must ransom the Holy Sepulcher from the infidels' hands, from the intellectuals of the faith, from the hands of those who have intellectualized the Christian faith. Faith is the religious experience of justice. It is the religious concomitance of justice. The person of faith will suffer for not being able to have more faith. "Increase our faith" and "atone our sin" is the same prayer. Faith will seek "only the Kingdom of Heaven and its justice." Faith will suffer for the injustice already wrought. For that reason the cross is an integral part of Christian faith. We must liberate the Church from the Pharisaic intelligentsia who hold it captive.

Although Bultmann and others - such as Käseman - maintain that faith falsifies itself when it converts itself into a "concept of the world, into a cosmovision," when it intellectualizes itself as if it were an ideology, faith does incarnate itself as its "Author and Consumer" Himself became incarnate. In this case to "intellectualize" does not have the same connotation that we gave it above. Upon incarnating itself, faith assumes a body of human rationality which will correspond to "the hope for justice" in a determined moment of history and to a social praxis which will manifest itself by loving and solid service for one's neighbor.

Biblical scholars almost unanimously agree that we find the purest concept of Biblical faith in Isaiah. In Isaiah 28:16-17 we read, "behold, I am laying in Zion for a foundation, a stone, a tested stone, a precious cornerstone, a sure foundation. Those who believe will not be in haste. And I will lay justice to the line, and righteousness to the plummet..." Paul himself declared, "The promise to Abraham and his descendants, that they should inherit the world, did not come through the law but through the righteousness of faith"

(Romans 4:13). The liberation of the Church from its Pharisees and their kind - the Saducees and Herodians - is determined then by its compromise with worldly justice, with social
liberation, neither more nor less.

These are the elements which in our Cuban experience
characterize the mutual genesis of evangelization and
politics.

Evangelization and Politics: Mutual Control

Here we use the word "control" with the meaning of "examination," "revision." Evangelization examines politics.
Politics revise evangelization. Whenever evangelization
ceases to be controlled by politics, the message of the
Gospels deteriorates, becomes distorted.

There is no doubt whatsoever that the verb "to evangelize" is also reflexive. It cannot be affirmed dogmatically,
since it is a generalized abstraction. The loving action of
faith which politics is, will always precede evangelization
as "Kerygma." Politics is never perfect.

At the same time politics does not depend on evangelization in order to be good. It is through the failure of
Christians and their Church to have faith in the loving action
of politics, that we are led to evangelize ourselves.

The present crisis in evangelization arises whenever it
converts itself into a methodology which makes the "acceptance of faith" possible, ideally for an "infidel." Faith then
becomes a mere "credential," with no critical meaning. One
recites the creed and memorizes Bible passages quite aside
from political, economic and social realities.

The Church believes it is fulfilling its mission to "go
and make disciples among all nations" simply by increasing
the number of baptisms and parishioners on its membership
lists. The Church has not realized that evangelization depends on the loving activities which we call political.
Evangelization converts itself into the means of expanding
the hegemony of a particular sect. Thus evangelization, when
it ceases to control the political activity of the believer,
converts itself into something "spiritual." Evangelization
is then reduced into the mere propagation of an "idea," the
defense of a "creed," the indoctrination of a "dogma." It
then ceases being the critical examination of the believer,

of politics; and it becomes a "ticket to heaven" for all believers. There are credulous people, and, there are true believers.

Politics control evangelization; otherwise it departs
from concrete reality. Is the task of evangelization perhaps
the same in socialist Cuba as it was in capitalist Cuba? The
same in the United States as in any nation of the so-called
Third World? In the German Federal Republic as in the Soviet
Union? In Viet Nam as in Chile? Certainly not. Politics-
loving activity of faith - performs distinctively different
types of action in each case. In Cuba we believers have had
to learn this. In today's world the Church cannot evangelize
with its back turned to the realities of ongoing revolution.
In Cuba, the Church cannot overlook the role which the Cuban
revolution is playing in the arena of the international proletariat.

Today the repudiation of capitalism as a system and the
frank option for socialism as the only road to liberation, is
the only loving activity which is valid and implicit in a genuine Christian faith. Whenever this road is taken by Christians and militants, it necessarily becomes a factor of un-
suspected weight in the process of renewal and reform which
the Church needs.

The Church must gradually enter the struggle in favor of
the poor and the exploited, in opposition to the exploitation
of person by person. The Church must speak out against private ownership of the means of production; against the lust
for profits at the cost of one's neighbor, such as motivates
people under capitalism.

The evangelical option of the Church today is none other
than to join the struggle of those working for a social appropriation of the means of production. The Church must
struggle for an effective participation of the masses in the
decision-making process. And the Church must join in the
realization of the historical project of socialism based
legally upon the establishment of representatives of the
working class, who will permit further progress towards a
society structured on the foundation of the elimination of
class antagonisms and the rise of the "new human being."

This Church will be united and indivisible because, as
we shall discover, the divisions now existing among Christians
are the same as those which divide the general populace. In

a world divided between exploiters and exploited, oppressors and oppressed, only the struggle in solidarity with the exploited and oppressed for the liquidation of all class divisions in society – only such a struggle will operate in favor of the definitive unity of the Church.

The Church must purge itself of its own sins; and the task of liberation in matters of conscience is not easy. Within the framework created by the bourgeoisie – especially in ideology – we are still prisoners. The reactionary ideology of religious faith is provoking a kind of "instrumentalization complex." Among a significant number of Christians who want to be revolutionaries, they have the feeling of being "manipulated." This psychic phenomenon produces a new ideological blockage to revolutionary commitment and gives rise to a subtle divisionism, unless it encounters a critical, timely solution. This ideological weakness can lead to a blind acceptance of a guilty conscience or to feelings of being "rejected."

The Cuban Church will have to renounce every kind of "psychic" complex and then, with complete freedom – the glorious freedom of the Children of God – press on for its own renewal, which, to my mind, will be on three levels. Let me elaborate on these three areas of renewal based in Christian freedom.

The first level is that of "faith." Here we are speaking about theological renewal. Theological renewal begins with a rediscovery of – or better said, a re-encounter with – the God of Biblical revelation. The Father of our Lord Jesus Christ is rediscovered. This encounter will clarify, once and for all, whether the God who is revealed in Jesus is revolutionary or counter-revolutionary. Is God a God of the poor and the oppressed, or is God a God of the rich and the exploiters? Is God with the Marxist who sacrifices his/her life for friends and neighbors, or is God with the "fascist" Christians who rob their brothers and sisters in violence?

The second level of renewal is that of "hope." This concerns the "pedagogical" renewal of the Church. Pedagogical renewal means returning to the rationality of faith in order to learn once and for all whether the Kingdom of Jesus, the Kingdom of God to which we look forward, is an anti-scientific absurdity or a hope that can be rationally accepted. This stage of renewal will clarify whether the Kingdom of God

is an erruption of a mechanized God, a monstrous clever trick
of some divine magician of the future, deceiving a great majority of humankind, or the natural result of the seeds we
have planted, the rational harvest of the fruits of our efforts. This Kingdom of God will be no mystery because of its
grandeur. "Hope against hope" becomes marked within an historical rationality and, therefore, is dialectic. For example
the "law of history," which speaks of the provable and proven,
takes on another dimension. That is to say, answers for the
ordinary questions take on other dimensions expanding our
understanding of historical possibility and dimension. For
example, Is Salvador Allende dead or alive? Are the only ones
alive the fascist assassins of Allende, the Chilean people and
their instigators of the CIA linked to exploitative, genocidal
imperialism? Or is there another set of answers here that
help us understand historically who is alive?

And, finally, the third level of renewal - the third to
note, but the first in importance - is love, "the greatest of
these." Here we speak of the love which has to do with the
political renewal of the Church. This love enables the Church
to return to just and precise action, to humanizing action.
Love speaks about what humankind is doing, not beasts, spirit
nor flesh, but people. This love does not preoccupy itself
with demons. This love involves the making of history, not
the realization of fantasy. This love enables the Church to
become the Church, not a sect. It becomes the faithful remnant, and not the assassin of God. Indeed, it becomes the
body of Christ, not the anti-Christ. For all this it will be
necessary to meet together anew in daily action confronted by
the truth that "God made people and put them in the garden of
Eden so that they might labor for it and take care of it."
And of this Jesus said, "My Father labors and I labor." We
will have to quit being the kings and queens in order to become the slaves. We must stop being served, in order to
serve. No longer can we be the exploiters and the oppressors.
We must be of the proletariat.

In other words, the Church must rediscover its own self
in the worker who dies today, assassinated for defending pro-
letarian rights, his own rights as a laborer, as a creator,
as a constructor. The Church must seek its rights as a worker
and not as an hierarchical ecclesiastic which considers itself
under the palladium asking for peace while it gorges on the

funds from the collections which arm the fascists and assassinate the workers, funds stolen from these very workers, "to be able to sell it, and later, to buy it for a pair of shoes."

These are the three permanent levels for the renewal of the Church:
- that of FAITH, i.e. of theology.
- that of HOPE, i.e. of pedagogy.
- that of LOVE, i.e. of politics.

Of these the greatest, most important, fundamental and decisive is politics, the one having to do with love which proletarianizes us. It is love which makes us people of creative labor; which makes us gather two or more together, in Thy Name. In the name of God we come together as brothers and sisters, as comrades. Like those of Emmaus, saddened by what they had heard, we shall be able to relate with joy "the events which befell us on the road" and how we knew it when we became "comrades," that is to say, sharers of our common bread.

These are the elements which, from our Cuban experience, characterizes the mutual control of evangelization and politics.

Evangelization and Politics: Mutual Verification

We use the word "verify" here in the most strictly accepted meaning of the Latin verus, as true, and facero, make, "probe the truth of something which is doubted."

In this sense evangelization verifies itself through politics and, vice versa, politics verifies itself through evangelization. We cannot forget that the historical subjects of evangelization are the poor. The poor who realize that their poverty is at the service of the cause of the poor, the humble, the oppressed, the weak of the world, these are the ones who are the subjects of evangelization. All the rest is pure demagoguery, however much disguised by evangelical verbosity.

On the other hand, tell me what politics you are accomplishing by really effective action, and I will tell you what kind of an evangelist you are. We cannot forget that the mediation of politics of evangelization is its true "sign and prodigy."

From our Cuban experience I must note the 1977 Confession

of Faith of the Presbyterian-Reformed Church of Cuba, as an
example of how evangelization and politics verify one another
mutually. In this document the following is affirmed:

This testimony constitutes the affirmation of the
joy which the Church of Jesus Christ experiences in
the Gospel as it lives this historic moment of humanity and especially as it proclaims the meaning
faith has for us in the midst of the Cuban revolutionary process.

God's Incarnation in Jesus of Nazareth and the
liberating vocation this fact implies for the Church
constitute the spiritual foundation for the historical commitment to which the Church feels it is
called.

It is necessary for the Church to clarify the
meaning of that commitment. As it does this, the
Church gives the reason for its hope and lives its
love confessing in this way its faith.

Obligated to carry out that commitment, the
Church, by the Spirit and through its own action,
is nourished by the knowledge it needs to have about
God's redeeming purpose in Jesus Christ as it is revealed in the Scriptures, norm of its faith, paradigm for its action.

When the Church lives its love for "Jesus Christ
and Him crucified," it takes on in full responsibility the solution presented by God to the human
problem through sacrificial and solidary love
which works justice and establishes peace.

The Church recognizes that sacrificial, solidary
and unconditional Love is necessary for it to be the
Church of Jesus Christ; and, espousing the cause of
human dignity and decorum in every moment and in
whatever place as its only reason for being, without
placing any condition on its commitment, and without
having it matter what the circumstances are in which
it lives or the risks which it runs, it participates
fully in human Redemption.

When the Church lives like this, it is living in
God, by God and for God. To serve and love God in
Jesus Christ is for the Church to center its inter-
est, its concern and its evaluation of all things in

the human being, accepting that the Christological
form of being is the only way for God to make Himself accessible to the Creature and the only way
for the Church to make itself acceptable to God and
to other human beings.

When the Church lives its historical reality placing the human being in the very center of its interest in Jesus Christ, it does not lose its identity as the "Body of Christ" or as "Christ's bride,"
but all the contrary; even in its greatest degree
of secularization the Church achieves the realization of its irrenunciable commitment of serving and
loving Jesus Christ, since in Him, at His own expense, God is secularized radically and unconditionally in his redemptive task of working for the
fullness of the decorum and dignity of all human
beings.

The Church, in its members, lives the community
action (KOINONIA) of the Holy Spirit that makes us
"companions" (KOINONOS) of our brothers and sisters
and God's co-actors in the task of human redemption, when said members are realized as "faithful"
economes before God and before their neighbors.

The Church lives in a real and concrete practice of human freedom on the part of the members
as they become committed participants in the quantitative growth and the qualitative development of
"love-justice" in the social, political and economic structures of human society, including the very
structures of the Church as a social-juridical
institution.

The Church lives its Love centered in the human
being, in the measure in which its members really
become a "community of economes" who feel responsible before God to try to live their condition of
human beings genuinely in complete fulfillment of
their responsibilities in the Redemption of Nature,
History and Human Conscience.

The Church lives in the militant and committed
participation of each one of its members in the task
of the integral reconstruction of the human being.
This reconstruction touches each person in his/her

spiritual, social, economical and ecological totality.

The Church lives in its members when they contribute in a real way and with concrete historic actions to the disappearance of the "old Adam," disintegrated by "sin" and "death." The Church realizes thus - and not in any other way - its true Catholicity and Apostolocity as the "Body of Christ," "the Bride of the Lamb," the "People of God," according to the evangelical teaching.

The Church lives in its members when they, faithful to the Gospel and to their Lord and knowing that it is not possible to serve two masters, repudiate service to God-Money. The Church is thus freed from the oppressive power with which the ideologies of domination and exploitation to this day have kept it captive, especially when under the imperialist political-cultural power, the Church is aware of how the greatest enemies of the human being today, and therefore, the greatest enemies of God, try to use it to defend their anti-Christian interests.

The Church lives in the same measure in which each one of its members works for the social-economic reconstruction of the human being within the Socialist State, because of all the historical forms of State known and experienced to this day, it is the society organized with socialist structures which offers the most concrete possibilities for making workable a more and more fairly distributive justice, which progressively reaches all citizens with greater efficiency.

The Church joyfully lives in the midst of the Socialist Revolution, since the Revolution has concretely and historically inaugurated a series of values in human relations that make possible the whole modern technical-scientific development at the service of the full dignity of the human being.

The Church lives this new situation without fears, proclaiming the truth of the Gospel, confiding only in its Lord and captive only of Jesus Christ. In that way it finds its place in the

human-historical process of integral recuperation.
To do this the Church does not begrudge any sacrifices that may be necessary to fulfill its mission,
whose special characteristics vary in accordance
with the moment and the place it has to live.

The Church lives through the concrete love
practiced by its members when they serve the socialist society without hostility, trusting the
divine-human sense of History and trusting the
future which envisions a more effective peace among
nations and a more real justice among human beings.

The Church lives in the responsible participation
of its members in the construction of the New Society through all its activities: in the Committees
for the Defense of the Revolution, in the Labor
Unions, in the Federation of Cuban Women, in the
Organizations of Pioneers, of Students, of Peasants;
in every effort and work carried out to create a
new society of producers and not just consumers,
where there is a place therefore for the creation
of a new kind of human being, for whom love is no
longer a Sunday morning commandment, but rather the
law which governs all daily actions.

The Church lives in the responsible and committed
work of its members who join in the struggles to
halt the present arms race, to achieve the total
disappearance of all testing of weapons for mass
destruction and the establishment of complete disarmament in the world. In a world where there exist
a United Nations Organization and a Helsinki Accord
of Pacific and Cooperative Relations Among Nations,
it becomes necessary for all government and non-
government organizations to make a special effort
to guarantee all peoples the achievement of their
full and responsible participation in the creation
of a world which is more just and more nobly human.
The Church is called to take part in this effort
because of its very Nature and Mission.

The Church lives concretely in the intimate relations which exist between the coming of Jesus
Christ the Savior and the definitive achievement
of "Peace on Earth among People of Good Will,"

the announcement of His coming.

The Church "prophesies" when it lives, in each
one of its faithful, the triumph of love over un-
love, justice over exploitation, truth over injustice, peace over competition, decorum over human
indignity. The Church lives "prophetically" in its
members when they become committed participants in
the death of the capitalist society and the dehumanizing and decrepit values it represents. Otherwise
the Church would be converted into a "scandal" for
God and a reproach for people, and its "destruction
will not be long in coming" like that of all false
prophets.

The Church prophesies when its members joyfully
live the feelings and actions of growing solidarity
of our socialist people for all the peoples of the
world. The Church prophesies when it expresses its
joy for the evident fact that this deep feeling of
solidarity is becoming a generalized characteristic
of the common citizen.

These are the elements which, in our Cuban experience,
characterize the mutual verification between evangelization
and politics.

*   *   *

EVANGELIZATION

IN THE CONTEXT OF BUILDING

THE NEW SOCIETY OF ANGOLA

EMILIO DE CARVAHLO

I shall first express my thanks to Dr. Sergio Arce Martinez for the friendly invitation he sent me to present a study
on "Evangelization and Politics within the Angolan Context"
before the participants in this consultative meeting of theologians of the Latin American and Caribbean Christian Peace
Conference. The pressures of my pastoral duties and the short
notice of the meeting both prevented me from preparing a longer report on what is happening in our country in this respect.

For us the theme is new. It dates from 1975. Previously
it was not discussed. Now, the churches are emerging from
the battlefield into the field of theological reflection.
The Biblical concept of salvation is being completed by in-
suring that the concept of "liberation" as a socio-political
phenomenon is examined.

The presentation of the liberating message of Christ to
the people of Angola (evangelization) began with the arrival
of colonialism in the fifteenth century. Missionaries and
imperialists arrived together, and in certain respects were
confused in the exercise of their respective missions. The
fundamental reason for this "evangelization" was to extend
the defense of the faith in the empire.

Missionaries during this epoch did not understand that,
in order to evangelize a people, it is essential first to
understand their political, economic, social and cultural
history.

In the nineteenth century, with the explosion of the
missionary movement, many missionaries thought arrogantly of
the Africans as "barbaric tribes waiting to be evangelized
and civilized," or as "depraved, denaturalized people who
could be helped by the blood of Christ of the Christian
Bible." Such regeneration of the African soul by colonialism
found acceptance of the evangelical message by the Angolans,
without doubt. It was carried by the missionaries under the

protection of the colonial State. Tragically, the Angolans'
faith was dominated by this colonialism as well. Their faith
became dominated by the religious oppression of their "older
brothers and sisters." Their regeneration of the "African
soul" taught us to hate what was really ours and to love what
was white. And much more happened during these years of colonialism. Portugese colonialism not only suffocated the appearance of the "African religious conscience," in their colonies, but also, through its utopian politics of assimila-
tion, Portugese colonialism sought to eliminate every variety
of cultural and political manifestation which arose automa-
tically from the people.

Thus colonialism was as much mental as spiritual. One
could speak only of "salvation from sin," and therefore the
salvation process was never ended. The illusory colonial
ideas limited salvation to the soul of the African pagan
and never dealt with the totality of the human being. Thus
the Church gradually suppressed all who were not Roman Catholic.

Today the situation has changed. Angolans, mentally de-
colonialized, want to communicate directly with God. They
no longer want mediation nor interference by the white co-
lonialists. As Bishop Potter says, "True evangelization is
not a copy of foreign forms for accepting Christ." The
Christian people of Angola intend to rediscover their African
identity. Thus, in our context, evangelization is related to
the de-colonialization of the Church, to the reformulation
and correction of its methods for evangelization. This reformulation covers all aspects of previous methods - theological, liturgical, structural, cultural. From this arises
the political aspects of evangelization in THE NEW SOCIETY.

This places the foreign missionary of today's Angola in
a deep dilemma. The dilemma carries him/her to spiritual
desperation, since s/he can no longer utilize the same instruments and arguments for evangelization. These outdated instruments are incapable of conveying the message in a language
intelligible to Angolans. The missionaries reach the conclusion that their God and their baptism will not extinguish
African beliefs (which they depreciatingly call pagan and
superstitious). These missionaries must now accept that
Africans are also a people of God, created in God's image.
They must accept that the African people are no longer pagan

as they had thought. The African people have always had the
capacity to BELIEVE which has enabled them to accept the new
faith. Today this faith turns them to seek a Christian mission relevant to our CONTINENT. The terms have become reversed. Thus, "The Church in Africa is not advancing in the
liberation process of the oppressed, since it also wants to
evangelize the former colonizers." This is called "transforming the Church of Christ in Africa, past creator of colonialism, into A CHURCH, as a genuine element of faith
which includes Jesus Christ." This new situation obliges
the boards of foreign missions which came to Angola in the
nineteenth century to seriously revise their thinking of
missionary work in the new Angola. In today's Angola mission
gives way to A CHURCH and the Gospels no longer serve as an
element of oppression but as an instrument of liberation.

The African identity which we are recovering requires an
Africanization of the Angolan Church. The Angolan Church desires to realize itself and develop itself, by itself. It
desires to apply the cultural values which will vitalize a
Gospel free of the stigma of "superstition."

Thus, evangelization has as its objective the establishment of a contextual Church. This will be a Church free of
theological ties and the tutelage of foreign missionary
boards.

In that context one must ask whether an "African theology of liberation" still exists in Angola. It was impossible
to speak of such a subject during the five centuries of colonialism. So, evangelization was an evangelization of peace-
ful co-existence, of survival.

The foreigners made attempts in the past to do theology
for us. But what we really had was a struggle for liberation
which oppressed people themselves had to carry out. This
sort of theology is beginning now. We see it happening in
individuals, in the Church structure, in the reformulation
of liturgies, in transmitting the life of the people. We
conclude that the total process of saving (evangelizing) the
Angolan people is becoming the liberation – political, economic and social – of all the forces of oppression which have
been impeding them from living like human beings; and the
Gospels are in the struggle against racism, colonialism and
exploitation. All that is evangelization.

Therefore, to evangelize, in the meaning of the building

67

of a new Angolan society, means to rediscover the social dimension of the Gospels. Prior to 1975 that rediscovery (in
concrete terms of activity) was prohibited. Whatever kind of
"African theological liberation" exists in Angola, it will
have to consider the exploitation suffered by the people for
five-hundred years and to struggle to eliminate the injustices
replacing them with justice and peace. By showing active solidarity with the people, the Christian converts him/herself
into a politician. S/he is "evangelizing." And this solidarity of the Church with the oppressed people in their struggle
for national liberation is an integral part of their program
of evangelization. It is a serious option.

On the other hand, the integration of the Angolan
Church into the improvement of living conditions is another
chapter in evangelization.

This redefinition of the mission of the Church in a society which is in a process of "decolonialization" is political. We do not support a theology of alienation, but one
of integration (CARR). We evangelize in order to obtain a
more abundant life in Jesus Christ in a just society, in
which the economic structures of exploitation are being dis-
mantled; in which all socio-cultural patronage is suffering
profound transformation. We are living in a society in
which barriers of race, culture and class erected by colonialism are being destroyed.

As I have said, evangelization in Angola began with the
arrival of colonialism. The sectarian nature of Protestantism served the colonial policy of "divide and conquer" since
it encouraged a paternalistic domination and intensified
tribalism, which divided us. Today evangelism is no longer
divisive, and the Angolan Council of Churches (CAIE) is now
a force of Christian unity.

The fundamental question is not how to transmit Jesus
Christ to the Angolans. Rather, it is to know whether Christians in Angola are evangelizing as Christ evangelized. And
to know whether the activity of evangelization is able to
make an effective radical change in the human condition.
Evangelization has to do with how the churches can "read the
political signs of the times." Evangelization challenges
churches which are still integrated with oppression to convert themselves into living testimonies of the integrity of
the Gospels. This evangelization is occurring in a revolu-

tionary society which is emerging from colonialism into a new
struggle against neo-colonialism, which intends to perpetuate
itself in the same missionary camp.

The freedom we are building in Angola does not limit the
constructive activities of the churches to the altars of its
rustic chapels. As Bishop Manas Buthelezi says, "The place
for serving God is not only in church sanctuaries, but also
in the dust and dirt of cities' daily life, where tears are
frequently shed and hopes are dashed."..."The Church is also
in Soweto." We think so too.

I am failing to report specific examples of the prophetic
integration of the Angolan Church (speaking of worldly, material things), such as are making us one of the most valiant and
faithful communities in Africa. These examples would speak
for themselves as cases of victory and defeat, giving testimony to the force of Christians engaged in building the new
Angolan society and in rediscovering the new Africa religious conscience. I do not know whether the sacrifice of so
many who have died for truth has been worth while. But the
truth is, that the Church of Angola will continue to intensi-
fy its evangelization as an instrument of liberation.

* * *

EVANGELIZATION AND POLITICS

FROM A GERMAN PERSPECTIVE

ILSEGRET FINK

My report is from a country which has been building socialism for the past thirty years. Thirty-four years ago we
were liberated from fascism by the allied armed forces.

I am a pastor with the Protestant Church of Berlin-
Brandenburg. My report will be limited to the role of the
Protestant Church; however, the Roman Catholic Church in my
country has played no better role than that of the Protestant Church.

My summary will attempt to be a simple overview of a
very complicated situation. What is important are not so
much the details, but the models of behavior which can be
seen.

Before discussing evangelization and politics in socialist Germany I must present an historical sketch. The conduct
of our Protestant Church under fascism and its attitude towards the socialist revolution is rooted in the position and
attitude of Martin Luther during the Peasant Wars of his day.

Christianity came to Germany from Rome during the first
century by evangelization. The Gospel of liberation through
Christ was preached, but in the fourth century the political
interests of the Roman State converted Christianity into a
state religion. This was done not through evangelization,
but by decree for the entire Roman Empire. The Emperor had
no interest in "liberation through the God of the Hebrews,"
nor in the faith of Jesus Christ. The Emperor needed a mono-
theistic religion in order to control the various rebellious
groups in the Empire.

Before the people had time to experiment with the func-
tions of evangelization as a liberating force, they experienced baptism as an arm of government. A Church-State was
set up very quickly; a clerical caste was established which
practiced religion through liturgies and the sacraments. Nevertheless, knowledge of the Bible, which was fairly customary
and habitual for the Hebrews, was not taught. The media for
evangelization were the sacraments, not the message of

70

liberation.

The monastic movement of the eleventh and twelfth centuries grew out of a critical reaction against the State religion. Members of religious orders wished to live strictly in accordance with the Gospel. Their vows of poverty amounted to an open critique of private property, but the Church accepted this critique neither in practice nor in its teaching. Subsequently the feudal powers of the monasteries made them so strong that, despite the poverty of the monks, they became part of the feudal system.

I mention this to bring out that Luther's critique of the monastic system was purely theological. He rejected the monastic life and all it stood for, because he saw no spiritual value in it; but when the Protestant princes expropriated the monasteries, Luther did not support the distribution of lands among the peasants. Thus the monastic lands fell to the Protestant princes. The Waldensians in Italy and the Brethren in Bohemia demanded the sociological and political consequences of the theology of the Reformation and thus received no support from the nobility. The noble lords would have suffered great losses if the Biblical interpretation of the Bohemian Brethren had been accepted at that time.

The evangelization of the Church during the Lutheran Reformation brought many positive changes. Christians were freed from the clerical dictatorship and the authority of the head of the family was greatly strengthened. From the translation of the Bible, the teaching of catechism and the Protestant hymns a great evangelization developed. This came one thousand years after the imposition of Christianity by force. The Roman Catholics too were affected by these changes.

The peasants, from their interpretation of the Bible, demanded the land which had not been give them. The peasant wars constituted the only liberation movement in Germany resulting from the inspiration of the liberation of the Hebrews from Egyptian captivity. These wars were a holy struggle against the feudal Church and the Christian landlords.

Luther did not obtain his concept of the theology of liberation from current social situations. In truth, he was far more involved in problems of Christology than in subdividing land among the poor. With his authority and his limited application of the Gospel he supported the counterrevo-

lution of the princes and denounced the revolution as a sin
against God. The peasants who were assassinated during the
religious wars by the "Christian" princes believed that the
Gospel represented true liberation. During the following re-
volts the revolutionaries believed that the Bible and the
Church were helpful only to the oppressors.

The first republic which was established after World War
I received no help from the Church because it was a product
of revolution. The failure of the Church to support the Wei-
mar Republic contributed, indirectly, to the rise of fascism.
The Church did not analyze incipient fascism, product of
Hitler's rhetoric, which spoke of the providence of God for
the German people. Even many theologians soon convinced
themselves of the positive nature of the new Nazi regime.

In 1934, for the first time since the Reformation of
Luther, the Church was confronted by the true Gospel. It was
a theological confrontation, not a critique or denouncement
of the evil nature of fascism, although this was already obvious in 1934.

The Swiss theologian Karl Barth, who recognized the need
for analyzing fascism and wished to help the Church in this
task, had to leave Germany in 1935 since the established
Church gave him no employment, fearing his anti-fascist attitude and stance.

Very few Christians entered the anti-fascist struggle.
The first manifestation of Christian-Marxist solidarity developed in fascist concentration camps. Prisoners of war
and officials, many of whom were Protestant ministers, organized the Committee for German Liberty in Soviet prison
camps in Moscow, as well as in the movement for German liberty in Switzerland. These people had personal contact with
communists, under very difficult conditions. They made some
cooperation possible later on, but they could not convince
the Church in its totality to accept the new situation until
1945.

The Declaration of Darmstadt in 1947 is the only document
of the Protestant Church of Germany which accepts its guilt,
openly and honestly, for the anti-revolutionary attitude of
the Church. Here is a quotation from the Declaration, "We
were mistaken in not listening to the voice of the poor and
not taking seriously the economic analysis of Marxism. We
opposed the revolution; more, we supported the growing drift

towards fascist dictatorship." But even this declaration of
the official Church was not strong enough to help the churches
of Germany start anew and avoid a basically anti-communist
attitude.

It is said repeatedly that problems arose in the German
Democratic Republic because there has never been a true socialist revolution; but history does not always follow classical models. Our socialist revolution was not made by poverty
as a revolutionary working class, but by liberation after
twelve years of counter-revolution against the German bourgeois democracy. In the Potsdam Agreements of 1945 the four
allied forces promised to remove fascism at its roots in
their respective occupation zones. For the communists this
meant, in the Soviet zone, the socialization of the means of
production, agrarian reform and educational reform.

Very soon the Protestant and Roman Catholic churches in
the Soviet zone of occupation were utilized from abroad for
anti-communist propaganda and activities. The churches were
considered poor, and received help from capitalist countries.
Gradually the churches became less convinced that socialism
would produce a greater amount of justice, since they had
lost many privileges. Nevertheless, many individual Christians participated actively in building socialism.

In 1958 Christians who felt that the Declaration of
Darmstadt should be expanded organized with their brothers
and sisters in neighboring countries the Christian Peace
Conference. The purpose was to call European churches to
repentance and to give witness to peace.

The Christian Peace Conference consists of a group of
Christians in the churches of eastern and western Europe
and was later expanded to include Asia, Africa and the Americas. This was the first time in Church history that Christians came together not only to support movements for social
reform but publicly supported revolution as a way to attain
a higher quality of justice. For the first time, Christians
announced that war and poverty are not inevitable, that both
can be eliminated. There are ten active sections of the
Christian Peace Conference in the German Democratic Republic. Lay members as well as clergy work on subjects such as
disarmament, peace in the service of youth, women's rights
and peace education.

The most important justification for or rationalization

of anti-communism is to protect Christianity. For the past
twenty years the Christian Peace Conference has been asking
Christians, especially in Europe and North America, to stop
justifying anti-communism, since it merely gives spiritual
backbone to the arms race.

Whoever becomes identified with the Gospels today and
favors the rights of the poor will find common cause with socialist and communist revolutionaries. Therefore the Fifth
All-Christian Assembly for Peace met in 1978 under the theme,
"God's Call for Solidarity."

I want to mention now the revolutionary patience exercised by our socialist state. Only one of our eight Protestant bishops cooperated at first with the new government.
Prior to 1969 the churches in the GDR were organizationally
united with those of the Federal Republic of Germany (commonly called "West Germany"). Our government had to wait
twenty years before the Protestant churches recognized the
GDR as a society. In order to preserve the unity of the
Church, those in the GDR wanted it to function in both of the
two antagonistic systems. Some thought that in this way they
might avoid the class struggle. But, what kind of evangelization could ever come out of a Church with a dual loyalty?
Despite the split, for twenty years the GDR continued urging
ministers and laity to help build socialism. This is extraordinary, since the world view and vision of the directors of
the communist party are atheist.

Our Christian party, the Democratic Christian Union,
tried to redeem the tradition of the early Christian so-
cialists and declared its solidarity with the communist party. Ten years ago, by the time the Church finally severed
its organizational ties with West Germany, some ministers and
professors of theology had been active for several years as
members of Parliament and the peace movement.

Many progressive activities have developed in our Church.
Clergy and laity participate in the ecumenical movement. Considerable research is going on in theology, Christian literature, sacred music. New churches are being built. The
Church owns libraries, bookstores, kindergartens, hospitals
and institutions for handicapped children. Sixty percent of
children with physical or mental handicaps are in institutions
of our Church. Evangelical academies are found in various
parts of the country. We participate actively in programs

74

against racism sponsored by the World Council of Churches,
and our Christian youth have collected funds for sending campaign tents to FRELIMO. We can think of no time during recent centuries when so many youth and intellectuals have participated in the life of the Church. They ask serious questions about the significance of the Gospels. But much remains still to be done to get us out of the ghetto of the
Church, and to increase our understanding of a responsible
participation in the life of our society. The fact that
many youths have pictures of Martin Luther King and Che
Guevara on their walls is no guarantee of their political
commitment. If one should ask them whether they support the
socialist revolution, a large proportion would note doubt
in their answers.

In sum, we must admit, in self-criticism, that our
churches did not contribute to the defeat of fascism nor
support the difficult beginnings of our German Socialist
Republic. During the blockade by West Germany, before we
were recognized by capitalist countries, our membership did
not support the revolution, but simply yearned, like the
children of the Hebrews in the desert, for the manna of Egypt.
Many just waited for liberation by capitalism and sought a
higher standard of living in the Federal Republic of Germany.
Today we too are affluent; still, the world economic crisis
has not stopped at the socialist borders. We are having new
economic problems. We are making some mistakes; but our
greatest problems are those arising from personal relationships within the new socialist society. There is a generalized problem between the people who lived under fascism and
through the early, difficult days of building socialism, and
those who have grown up in socialist society, taking all its
gains for granted.

Here for example is one of the questions we must ask ourselves: "How can we help youths in their identity crisis?"
How can we maintain the revolutionary impetus?

We have had no equivalent historical experience, so we
must develop new, original concepts and strategy. For example, we Christians are trying to influence those who publish
critiques of our society in the press of West Germany. We
suggest that rather this be done on the proper occasions in
our own country.

Never before has it been so necessary to interchange

ideas with Christians who have established proper connections between evangelization and politics. We must try to understand every special situation and, at the same time, the historical conditions which led to that situation. For, just as we have counter-revolution, we also have counter-evangelization.

Given the complexity of the world situation, Christians can be faithful to the common task only if they help one another to discern the Holy Spirit within us, in each person's soul, to see whether these are coming truly from God. Since we are totally dedicated to mutually awakening our consciences, more and more Christians are supporting revolutionary changes for justice, for peace and for contributing to the disarming of the counter-revolution.

Only this process and development, in time, will demonstrate whether the changes in our congregations today are really evangelization or whether, again, they may be opium for the people - in our case, specifically, opium for the affluent socialist society.

*　　　　*　　　　*

CHRISTIANS IN VIET NAM

FRANCOIS HOUTART

In the absence of Vietnamese Christians it is my duty to discuss this subject now. I shall try to do so as honestly as possible, within an analytical framework. I apologize for my inadequacies in the hopes that the information presented will be useful.

I. The First Evangelization

1) Tribute as the Means of Production, The Asian Means of Production

Viet Nam has been characterized by "tribute as the means of production," often referred to as the Asian means of production. This is fundamental for understanding the country's sociology and as a background for its religion. Feudalism also existed, but the main basis of the Vietnamese political and economic system has been tribute, until very recently.

We cannot go into the details of its beginning but to say that international commerce had a profound influence. It explains the great religions and their ethics along the trade routes between Persia and China - Zoroastrianism, Buddhism, Confucianism - all of which began at about the same time.

The Asian means of production means, essentially, interchange between a strong central state and the autonomy of independent local social units. The origin of this structure was, generally speaking, a result of the profits from trade, assured by the mercantile role of a group which thereby acquired a dominant position. Trade relationships were established which were unequal, or tributary, but having the fetish of equality. Protection against tribute also arose as a consequence of the unnecessary religious dicta of the basic social structure, as the means of feudal production.

This explains the power of the rural structure of Viet Nam, up to the present day; the basis of the guerrilla organizations and the territorial militias, as well as of the Americans' plans for destroying the sociological "infrastructure," including the forced migration of ten million people. It also explains the division between the popular religion, chiefly Buddhism and the religion of the elite, Confucianism. Finally it explains the continuity of ancestor worship.

2) Mahayana Buddhism (The Great Vehicle)

Contrary to Teravada Buddhism (Lesser Vehicle), which has always been related to power centers, through a fundamental alliance between the king and the sangha (monastic institution), Mahayana Buddhism has a popular character, not only as a protective religion but also as one of protest. Salvation (nirvana) is available to everyone, not to monks alone, as well as mediation, through the hodhisattvas - people who have almost reached nirvana and now pause on the way to help others. Also there is the mediation of a savior - a messiah - the Buddha Maytia. The sangha plays no political role, but helps in situations of crisis. In contrast Hinhayana Buddhism (lesser), which came to Campuchea with the Indian kings, was closely linked with privilege. Mahayana Buddhism came from the north through the trade routes.

Buddhism, as a popular religion, incorporated elements of Taoism and other pre-Buddhist religions; worship of spirits, animism and ancestor worship, as symbolic of social relationships, even as symbolic kinfolk heroes.

3) Christian Implantations

In Hinayana areas (Lesser Vehicle) Christianity never penetrated the masses, but only marginal areas, since it was entrenched in the fundamental economic fabric. In contrast, Christianity did penetrate more in countries with Mahayana Buddhism. Christianity entered Viet Nam in the sixteenth century from the Philippines with Spanish missionaries, also from Thailand with French missionaries. It preceeded overt colonialization during the mercantile expansion period, as in most of Asia.

Christianity encountered two main obstacles in the structure of tribute: a) The basic social identity of the masses - since Christian conversion signified a separation from the group, especially from ancestor worship and from belief in spirits and animism; and b) the central power structure of kingship saw a danger to its well integrated hegemony.

Consequently Roman Catholic villages were established, either through the conversion of an entire village or the resettlement of converts to form a new village. This explains concentrations such as a region in the north of lands reclaimed from the sea. Also there were several persecutions by political forces.

78

From the beginning a Vietnamese clergy was formed, at a seminary near the frontier. The Bishops were either Spanish or French. The persecutions gave the French a good pretext for intervention. A French Bishop mediated with the emperor, which led to the introduction of capitalist production in the protected areas.

The French made an alliance with the ruling elite without greatly changing the internal social structure, which explains why there was no constitution such as in the English colonies which has a western petit bourgeois character. Working class groups appeared on the plantations, in mines and in some consumer industries.

By the time of World War II Vietnamese Roman Catholicism was established among a majority of the peasants and fishermen. Also a few westernized middle class people, mostly through schools and universities, had become Roman Catholic. There were relatively few intellectuals. The clergy were both foreign and national. There were even a few Vietnamese Bishops under the age of thirty. It was a very "clerical" clergy not only spiritually but also socially. As an indirect result of the tributary political and economic system, this was particularly true in the Roman Catholic villages. The Church as an institution was powerful and it was protected by the colonial administration. The large plantations had also made the Church a wealthy institution.

II. The Struggle Against French Colonialism

The struggle against French colonialism grew rapidly, directed by the Indo-China communist party, which means that it was a struggle against the capitalist system. This presented the Roman Catholics with a double problem: the loyalty of most of the Bishops to France and the problem of atheism, which was represented by the Chruch as an absolute impediment to all collaboration.

It would take too long to report here on the historic development of the Roman Catholic situation. We shall record simply two events as indications. First, the bombardment of Haiphong in 1948, which started the second war with the French and produced 8,000 victims. It was directed by Admiral Thierry Argenlian, a Carmelite priest, then chief of the French Pacific fleet. Second, the visit of General Delattre Tassigny. When named as general delegate to Indochina

in 1951 he went first to Rome, where he made two requests of
the Pope: to name an apostolic representative in Hanoi and
to have the Vietnamese bishops issue a condemnation of communism. The Pope complied with both and then blessed the
French troops who were defending "Christian civilization" in
Viet Nam.

The deep dilemma of the Christians who were committed to
the anti-colonial struggle is understandable. On October 9,
1951, the Bishops excommunicated all Catholics who participated, directly or indirectly, in establishing the power of
the communist party. These Catholics formed a Committee of
Coordination of Patriotic Roman Catholics, which included
several priests.

But in the new war the French organized and armed militias in the French villages, often led by soldier-priests, to
fight against the Viet Minh - which finally won victory at
Dien Bien Phu. The accords of Geneva in 1954, which foresaw
changes in the two zones, resulted in the migration of 600,000
Roman Catholics from the north to the south - half of their
total number, including 75 percent of the clergy and all but
one of the seminaries - that of Vinh.

Entire towns went south, influenced by the armed militias,
under intense religious propaganda and aided by French and
American vessels, through fear of religious persecution. From
this time two different histories begin.

III. The Church of the North

With its very conservative tradition and fear of communism, the Church of the North enclosed itself in a ghetto.
The hierarchy and some of the clergy were stongly opposed to
socialism. Thier isolation and conflict lasted until 1973.

The agrarian reform of 1956 caused serious problems in
the areas of Catholic majority. In truth the authorities,
despite their desire for reconciliation, utilized the reform
for taking revenge against the Catholics. Therefore those
responsible were removed.

Nevertheless the Catholic masses entered progressively
into the process of socialist organization. The Americans
helped in this process because their bombing, which began in
1966, brought the Catholic resistance to an end: they integrated themselves wholly, or almost wholly, in the national
struggle for defense and social transformation.

Still the relations between Church and government remained strained. Disappointed that the seminarians had not returned from the south, the Bishops wanted to open new seminaries. The government asked them to use new textbooks in order to teach socialism, also that the teaching staff should include members of the Committee of Patriotic Roman Catholics, of which two-thirds of the clergy were now members. But these conditions were refused. The Seminary of Vinh alone remained open - until destroyed by American bombs. Only a few more than one hundred priests were ordained in the next twenty five years, for over one million Catholics.

The dialogue with the state did not stabilize; the condition previously demanded by the Bishops was the return of the national properties. The Bishops were not authorized to participate in Vatican Council II for fear of undesirable contacts with the south and with the west. This produced an even greater conservatism.

Lay Catholics and Protestants - there were no more than 10,000 of the latter in the north - entered into the struggle in large numbers, also into the administration of the country - as vice-ministers, parliamentarians, presidents of the Red Cross, etc. Churches were active and well attended, including men and youths.

IV. The Church in the South

The influx in 1954 brought the Catholic composition of the population to ten percent. They rapidly established well organized parishes, under strong clerical authority. They emerged in various regions, notably the suburbs of Saigon and several points on the highway between Saigon and Dalat, and the northwest.

The Diem regime was organized under American influence. Diem was called a Roman Catholic of the "Spanish type," as he himself said. He was presented to the American public by Cardinal Spellman. Supporting the American plan for building a capitalist society in the south, to be armed against the north and to be dependent economically on the United States. The new regime provoked an important social change.

A new bourgeoisie was constituted, in various sectors: a "buying sector" composed partly of Chinese elements and partly Vietnamese, associated with the regime; another sector was commercial, from large to small businesses, generated more or less by the war and the black market; a bureaucratic sector, and a military sector. Christians were numerous in all but the first and second sectors.

Diem utilized religion in the regime in two ways. He supported the Catholics and especially the immigrants from the north in organizing themselves. Thus a large proportion of military officers were Catholic recruits. It is interesting to note that Thieu converted to Catholicism at this time; that the Presidents of the Jury and of the House were Roman Catholic, as well as fifty percent of the members of the former and seventy percent of the latter. Catholics who had come from the north were sent back north as spies and saboteurs. Executive power under Diem became a family affair. His sister and his Aunt Nu exercised important power in social affairs, as well as the latter's husband. A brother was Archbishop of Hué and president of the Bishops Conference. Diem tried to become Archbishop of Saigon by the Pope denied him this.

Diem also utilized Christianity for building an ideology for his political system. Aided by a Belgian engineer, he developed "personalism" for his anti-communist ideology.

All this provoked strong reactions among the Buddhists, in certain pagodas particularly. Several monks immolated themselves in protest.

At the same time the Church as a whole was growing - in congregations, convents, sanctuaries, schools, works of all kinds; construction of a Sanctuary of the Virgin near the 17th parallel; increased missionary activities among the tribes (ethnic minorities); larger number of religious vocations for men as well as women; introduction of new practices such as the worship of Our Lady of Fatima, an anti-communist appearance of the Virgin; etc. All these developments took place during the twenty years from the Geneva Accords to the liberation of Saigon. Help from abroad was important, in both personnel and material support. During the American war we must remember also the visits of Cardinal Spellman and the commanding officer of the American army, who declared that the American soldiers were soldiers of Christ.

There was, however, an active minority of Catholic laity, the Catholic Worker Youth (JOC), some intellectuals and students, priests and monks, who opposed the regime of Diem, and later that of Thieu. Many were imprisoned, tortured and even

killed. These formed the principal group of the Christian
renewal following liberation.

V. The Liberation of the South

The process of liberation was very rapid, especially
around Saigon. Only those Catholics most closely associated
with the former administration, or those who had enriched
themselves sufficiently, were able to escape. The rest were
of two classes: groups of poor peasants and fishermen origin-
ally of the south, with a few urban workers. Groups origin-
ating in the north had become relatively affluent, through
hard work and help from abroad. These were still fairly
anti-communist except for the youth, who had not experienced
the journey from the north.

There was also a group of urban middle class Catholics
which had developed during the war. Sixty percent of the
schools were Church schools. All these Catholics enjoyed
little privileges which they feared losing under communism,
especially those employed in the administration, education,
the press, etc.

The clergy of the south were more affected by the re-
forms of Vatican II - in liturgy especially - and were more
open to change than in the north for the past twenty years.
Still they were quite clerical in the exercise of pastoral
missions, and they had a deep distrust of the new regime.

The religious situation was important for all, and was
closely bound to the identity of each group. The propaganda
of Thieu and the Americans had led them to expect a bloodbath
especially for believers. But this did not take place.
They had a pleasant surprise. Nevertheless, the pressing
economic problems, the low standard of living - no higher
than in Bangladesh - with the problems of re-education and
new orientation by popular assemblies- all this caused problems for everyone, not only for Catholics.

We must add that certain negative attitudes of the Roman Catholics did not help them make a favorable climate. For
example, eight days prior to the liberation of Saigon the
Papal Delegate appointed Mons. Nguyen Van Binh, the Archbishop of Saigon, as auxiliary Bishop with the right to name
his successor. This man was a nephew of Diem and was well
known for his militant anti-communism. There was a reaction
among progressive Catholics and violent counter-demonstrations

among rightist Catholics, with one death. Finally the government had to intervene by removing the Bishop, after two months of exercising patience. He was placed in his previous diocese. Since he continued to be active against the new regime he was imprisoned for several months and then appointed to a parish in the north.

Foreign missionaries were ordered to leave the new, progressive country. Some reacted by starting a vigorous campaign against Viet Nam from abroad, with other refugees, especially through "Radio Veritas" in the Philippines, financed largely by Catholics in the Federal Republic of Germany. A majority of the military chaplains were put into re-education camps, not for being priests but for being military officers. By the end of 1978 about one hundred of these were still there. Incidents took place, but were fairly isolated. In a suburb of Saigon, San Vicente, a press for counterfeit money and an arms depot were found. A group of friars and monks from several congregations were implicated in forming a clandestine government. But such incidents had little effect on the Catholic community.

Mons. Binh, Archbishop of Ho-Chi-Minh City, published two pastoral letters creating the "Episcopate of the South," a new board of bishops, because of the changed situation. He called on Catholics to integrate themselves into the process of reconstruction, reunification and the rebuilding of the country. In one of these letters Mons. Binh declared that socialism was closer to the Gospels that capitalism. In his official communication to the Roman Synod he affirmed that if Marxism is a challenge to Christians, it should be accepted.

Furthermore, the new Bishops' Conference's practices were consistent with its teachings. Catholic institutions for health and social training were integrated with the state. Only a few hospitals remain in the hands of the Church. Nuns and other members of religious organizations were asked to work in the new state social institutions such as the rehabilitation centers for prostitutes (more than 300,000 in the south), for drug addicts (about 500,000) and for orphans (about 400,000).

In the diocese of Ho-Chi-Minh City a large part of the state farmlands was entrusted to the Catholic clergy. Seminarians had to work for a year on the land before beginning their theological studies, as required by the Bishop. Priests,

monks and nuns volunteered their labor at various times. They
made retreats in this way. Some Catholic priests held important positions – professors and national legislators.

The Archbishop of Hué reacted against the changes in
his area, saying that Catholics were second class citizens.
But the authorities replied that obviously one could not think
of enjoying the same privileges as those of the previous regime. Religious practices were on a higher plane than before,
due to the situation of crises – and there were conversions.
One of the problems not yet settled is that of the missionaries among the ethnic minorities in the mountains. The former missionaries have not been replaced by native priests,
probably so as not to upset the delicate process of integrating these populations into the changes to socialism.

After three years of the new regime one may note the
following types of Catholic activists:

a) A small reactionary group of former militarists, refugees from the north, belonging mostly to the petit bour-
goisie, including some priests;

b) An expectant majority, satisfied that the religious
situation is not too bad but fearful of the future when the
regime would be more firmly established. A large part of the
clergy have this attitude and some of the parochial communities and intellectuals;

c) A group which accepts socialism but is centered on
the institutionalized Church. Because of this focus they
try to "save the Church" in the new situation. They are
very sensitive to certain limitations in religious activities,
such as the prohibition of pilgrimages, etc. and to incidences
of friction.

d) A group which is well integrated into the revolutionary process since it represents a process of liberation which
is an integral part of evangelization. This group directs
the Catholic Weekly, published in Ho-Chi-Minh City. It supports the publications of the Bishop, the Synod of Justice
and the theology of liberation.

Analyzing the dynamics of the situation, one notes a
progressive integration of popular Catholic elements into
the new society, not only through their ideological convictions but at least through practical necessity. The clergy
is integrating itself also, at least in Ho-Chi-Minh City, as
much through conviction as through solidarity with the populace.

The latter is the case especially among religious workers, who generally are closer to the poor and who see the efforts being made to solve the social problems of the country. The mental evolution of the clergy, somewhat slower, is important bearing in mind the traditional role of authority which they play in Catholic communities.

The new situation has produced a very deep transformation both internally and spiritually. The very conception of evangelization has been revised, although much remains to be done; and more, the practice and experiences of socialist perspectives in social and economic organization has been changed. The fact that many people work on the land, even for only a few days, indicates a revision, a profound change, in occupation. Would that this might make us feel more free!

All this does not mean that there are no incidents, as might be expected in such a complicated situation. Some Bishops and priests do not respond very positively. On the other hand some sections of the communist party occasionally take dogmatic, partisan positions – such has been the case with some of the sections which have come down from the north and have been absolutely essential for filling the administrative and political vacuum in the south. But many times they do not always understand the situations and mentalities of the south.

Conclusion

In summation, we may think that in the future there are possibilities for the improvement for cooperation between sectors of the Church and the developing socialist society. For example, we can assume that popular organizations of Catholics will integrate themselves more and more as they witness social and economic betterment. The natural catastrophies of the war and the subsequent economic problems have made this integration difficult to see as of yet. Such is the material basis for public opinion. But the fact that they are going to be able to express faith in progress has great importance. True, it is an ambiguous faith, allied with a yearning for protection in the facing of social change. And it is a faith linked to the social identity of one's group (each group is a minority group, constituted as part of a society with important elements still linked to the tributary means of production). But, being religious groups, they have coherent traditions vis-a-vis the persecutions of the previous century and other problems. Also they have a deep appreciation of God. This appreciation is expressed in their class status, but it can be integrated, little by little, in their objective place in the revolution.

Resistance is stronger in the middle class - where there is greater potentiality for intellectual leadership, as already noted. Its further integration in social and political change will depend greatly upon improvements in economic conditions and the progress of revolutionary change among the inhabitants of the south.

The clergy, while still an obstacle, may become (and already is, for a dynamic minority) an agent for change, because of its important influence in the smaller communities. The congregations of religious workers, especially those of Vietnamese origin, will play an important practical role, which can in practice be of considerable effect, because of the attitude of many Catholics, like that of many Marxists, who admire their openness and their capacity for hard work.

We can also imagine that the recent attack of China will stimulate the integration of Catholics into the national and social processes - similar to the effect of the American bombing in the north. Apparently they did not think of this!

Finally I wish to say that, despite all its problems, Viet Nam offers a great hope: not only for the prospects for Christians and Marxists working together and talking concretely together in this part of the world, but also of doing so on other continents as well. Our Christian and Marxist brothers and sisters in Viet Nam have a great responsibility, but these people have accustomed us to seeing miracles. I believe, for my part, that they will be capable of accomplishing their historical task, as they have done in so many other fields.

*   *   *

THE PRINCIPAL TASK

OF THEOLOGY TODAY:

AN INTERPRETATION OF THE
THEOLOGY OF LIBERATION

PAULOS MAR GREGORIOS

Many of our theologies of liberation are guilty of making "short circuits" in the Gospels. They are often based on
defective Christologies and ecclesiologies. They try stren-
uously to domesticate the Gospels within history, lacking
sufficient sensitivity to the transcendental dimensions of
both history and salvation. This is precisely where such
theologies should be revised: they should take seriously the
rejection by Jesus of searching for the path of mere political revolution, organizing the populace for armed struggle
against tyranny, imperialism and exploitation of Rome. His
path was not one of mere political insurrection, but rather
that of death and resurrection. If Latin American theologies
are to be taken into account seriously they must struggle for
the incarnation, the cross and the resurrection in a deeper
manner than what is implied by the fact that Jesus questioned
the existing structures of the Church and society. It is not
enough to state that He was partial to poor and marginalized
people. An appropriate ecclesiology can be constructed only
if the theologies of liberation make themselves profoundly
Christian.

As a Christian I would like to present a different approach to many of the theologies of liberation. Asians frequently encounter in these theologies a mere echo of European
culture. They often seem to have a basically Spanish-Portu-
gese orientation. They have tried - most inadequately - to
place themselves above the ancient pre-Colombian cultures of
the Americas. Millions of poor people in the Americas are
"latinos" or "Americans" only superficially. They are still
"Indians." Their cultural background is Mayan, Aztec, Incan,
Cherokee and African. A theology of liberation lacking roots
in these cultures must be foreign to the poor of this continent.

It is absolutely essential to have an understanding of and a sensitivity to the anthropology - including art, symbols, psychology and the forms of communication - of any people before endeavoring to carry liberation to them. This is particularly true as one approaches the "masses of the continent."

The most important key to liberation is vigilance lest indigenous cultures develop cosmologies or sociologies which are overly abstract or rational. Rather, a cosmology or sociology must express an understanding of the reality of a given people. It must touch their unconfessed aspirations, as seen in their folk symbols, music, etc. These may be at the same time cultural, religious and socio-economic. Due to their continuity and their persistence, our theologies of liberation must impress the indigenous American masses as dry and sterile. Religion must always be expressed by symbols, rituals and art forms which communicate more deeply than our abstract thinking and the rational "central categories" imported from the European Renaissance.

Last year I was greatly impressed by the crowds in the Basilica of Guadeloupe, in Mexico. They were not people on whom our theologies of liberation would have much effect. I remember particularly a youth, fervent in his piety, making his genuflexes before Our Lady of Guadeloupe. He was wearing a shirt bearing the image of Che Guevara. This is the combination found worldwide among the poor - a fervent revolutionary surrender united with an equally fervent devotion to the transcendental, expressed not by intellectual faith but through symbols and rituals which penetrate deeply into the subconscious.

Latin American theologies of liberation must take into consideration these fundamentals of continental consciousness in their message to the poor. They must learn to use something more than intellectual conceptions. The conceptual formulation of the theology should provide space for the trans-conceptual expression of the deepest aspirations of human beings. We must go beyond the pseudo-Marxist interpretations of the Gospels, which are neither Christian nor Marxist. I am posing polemics at this international meeting in order to provoke discussions. The urge to arrange a marriage between Christianity and Marxism impresses me as something artificial and unconvincing. Not only at its initiation must a theology of liberation be Christian. There is no

obstacle in learning something from Marxist scientific sociology and economics - provided that these elements are assimilated and thoroughly integrated. An understanding of modern
science and their theology, a deep understanding of the historic role of worldwide capitalist imperialism and the struggle against it by the oppressed and exploited of the world,
must be integrated with the Christian vision of the dynamic
process of creation-redemption in Jesus Christ. This appears
to be the task which we still must assume adequately and carry out rigorously, not merely in terms of Renaissance rationality and European cultural insularity.

A Christian theology of liberation should be rooted in a
community which lives for the mysteries of the incarnation,
death and resurrection of our Lord, and not merely in a sharing of poverty or readings about poverty in the Gospels.
There is no necessity for reducing the Gospels to these elements. It is sufficiently fruitful to provide full understanding of the dignity and the liberty of humanity, created
in the image of God, and at the same time to augment the categories of participation in the struggle for the emancipation
of humanity, without resorting to such dubious diminishment
of the Gospels.

A Genuinely Christian Theology of Human Totality

I recall sitting next to a distinguished Marxist intellectual at the only Christian-Marxist dialogue organized by
the World Council of Churches in 1938. After some of our
Christian theologians had made their presentations, he turned
to me and said, "You Christians are kind, recognizing all the
baggage which we Marxists have been writing about for fifteen
years and giving it back to us as Christian theology. Have
you no harvest of your own to give us?" I think we made a
mistake in trying to mix Marxism and Christianity. What we
need is a theology which starts out with an understanding by
Christians of creation, redemption and eschatological totality, and which places the struggle for socio-economic and
political liberation within the context of that totality. We
cannot begin with certain parts of the Gospels, arbitrarily
chosen, such as those of identification with the poor. The
faith of the Christian Church offers a prospect of reality
far deeper than what would fit into a concept such as identification with the poor, or Jesus the revolutionary. We

90

need not abandon our faith in Christ as the Incarnate Son of
God, His death and resurrection and continuous labors for human
redemption in order to be participants in the revolutionary
struggle for the emancipation of humanity from its oppressive
socio-economic and political structures. We do not need to
identify the Kingdom of God with the Church in order to be
faithful to the Gospels. What we need to do is to give ourselves a deeply Christian perspective which includes salvation
for the non-believer, baptism and faith, of a Christology,
spirituality and eschatology which places justice amidst the
greatness of a dynamic creation advancing towards its totality. Such a Christology, spirituality and eschatology can be
faithful to traditions and related to the emancipation and
redemption of not only the totality of humanity, but of the
entire universe. However, at the same time, it cannot be
wholly rational or intellectual. We must make use of symbols,
rituals and other trans-conceptual devises.

The Integration of Politics and Economics in such a Theology

I am allergic to the concept of evangelization as an "all
inclusive" category in which our political, economic and social worries are integrated. These can be integrated properly
only within a Christian containment of creation and redemption
in Jesus Christ as understood to consist of a cosmic phenomenon within the movement by which creation advances. The
class struggle, the development of human organization through
slavery, feudalism, capitalism and socialism, the present role
of imperialist capitalism and the present status of the struggle against its structures - all this can be contained within
the broad movement of creation towards its totality. This
should require an understanding and inclusion of the person
and the works of Christ, of the Holy Spirit and of the Church.
This needs to be oriented towards the redemption of all creation, not merely of Christians. Such is the great task of
modern theology, and one can note an element which is dis-
loyal to the traditional, the authentic, the classical positions of the Church. This task of modern theology will
obviously be of a different strain that the majority of the
theological currents most frequent in both the West and the
East. Politics and economics do not necessarily lie outside
of this theology.

Christian theology ought to provide not only a coherent

tentative sketch of reality. But Christian theology should also demonstrate how this reality can be changed.

Humankind is situated at the head of creative activity. This should be understood for what it constitutes not only because of this work but also because of the use it makes of its liberty for changing its status. In this the authentic tradition insists upon five points:

1) That humanity is an integral part of creation as long as it is able to transcend and modify creation;

2) That hand in hand, theory and practice, the individual and society, reflection and action, spiritual growth and the development of solid justice, must be coordinated;

3) That Jesus Christ, present in the Spirit of the Church, in society and in the cosmos in different ways, is active, as we are by this work. Jesus Christ is maintaining and nourishing this intuition in the life of the Church through the Eucharist and other symbols, as well as through instruction. Furthermore, affirmation of the hope that Christ and goodness will triumph over evil which will vanish, will be maintained by the Church;

4) That throughout history the final separation of good from evil can be made only partially, but that the final eschatological reality of the good, purged of evil, and ever growing to new dimensions, ought to exist in history as far as possible; and

5) That redemption in Christ must be made effective not only for humanity, but also for the totality of creation, even though this be effective in three different ways – politically, economically and socially – which cannot be understood as alien to Christian interests.

Some Specific Tasks for Christians Today

It would be superficial to assume that the Church as a whole will be faithful to the totality of its vocation. The official Church is constantly complying with some of its tasks while disdaining others, and frequently is on the path to genuine liberation and social justice. Thus the Church should often be called to the orders of believers, but one's critique of the Church could be too slow and too unproductive. Some of its tasks can be undertaken by only certain individuals or groups within the totality of the Church.

Let us give several examples of this.

1) The Church has a pastoral role to play in the revolutionary process. Revolutionaries need the support of the Church even when it does not share in their activities. Frequently this task may be performed successfully by small groups within the Church;

2) The Church should lose all its fear of interpreting political, economic and social realities. But often the Church is impeded from seeing reality because of its own created interests and therefore it does an inadequate job of interpretation. Again, unofficial groups in the Church will have to undertake this task;

3) The Church has the role of "giving names to the forces of evil" and practicing exorcism over them. This might force the Church to be crucified and the official Church is often afraid of the cross. Small groups will have to face those wicked powers and carry the cross in the name of the whole Church and all of humanity;

4) The Church should be free, since faith and hope will help us to see the role which certain interests play, and which impede us from facing reality. Frequently in many such situations the Church is so involved with its own interests and egotistical institutional efforts that it offers only a negative testimony. Small groups can make it clear to Christians how it is that they are really bound to their interests and therefore incapable of seeing reality as it is. Small groups can denounce the ideological chains which imprison believers;

5) The Church should help humankind challenge the questionable attainments of science and the propagandistic claims of much that passes for science, for example, in the fields of sociology, political science and economics. But the institutionalized Church many lack the courage to defy the status quo. Small groups must undertake the task of denouncing, for example, questionable economic concepts such as those of Walt Rostaw (stages of economic development), John Kenneth Galbraith (works on industrial society) or Vassily Leontieff (economics of computors); and

6) The Church itself might fear supporting revolutionary movements or parties, or to offer them their favor. It can therefore be the task of small groups in the Church to evaluate these movements and parties in a just manner. Then support and encouragement can be offered.

This list might be continued, but the central point is that the main task in theory and practice is the task of small groups in the Church. We ought not to reject this task, nor fear identifying ourselves with secular movements for liberty and social revolution. Nor should we fear cooperating with them in solidarity. The role of an adequate theology of liberation is that of serving in this task.

*　　　*　　　*

EVANGELIZATION AND POLITICS

A BRITISH CARIBBEAN PERSPECTIVE

ERNLE P. GORDON

For over three hundred years the process of evangelization and expansion of the Christian Church in the British
Caribbean coincided with the political, economic, social and
cultural expansion of Great Britain. The Christian churches
in the British Caribbean have been continuously exposed to
these external influences. Caribbean societies whose economic systems are traditionally dependent on the taste and
preferences of alien people, have imported values through a
series of foreign contacts, culminating in hopes and dreams
that are oriented towards North America and Great Britain.

The evangelical process disregarded the complex nature
of Caribbean societies, failing to utilize the richness of a
cultural creativity which abounded so plentifully in countless
Caribbean cultural mores, norms and folk ways. There have
been attempts to indigenize the medium of evangelization, but
most of the music is Gospel music from the United States of
North America and the accent of the preachers is also strictly North American. The economic system has created a Caribbean person who is a product of slavery, feudalism and capitalism. To create a new person is not an easy task for the
Church in the Caribbean, which itself needs to be liberated
from "psychological slavery." It is like when Moses tried
to free the Hebrews from Egyptian exploitation. He soon
discovered that, their minds were so converted to Egyptian
slavery that when they were hungry they preferred to return
to Pharoah's bondage. Many Caribbean church leaders and politicians have learned that to change the psyche of Caribbean people distorted by slavery is a very difficult one. No
wonder Bob Marley wrote, "Emancipate yourself from mental
slavery."

Therefore, the Caribbean has been a pawn throughout its
history in struggles for power, first European and now North
American. Gordon Lewis described this situation very well in
his brilliant work The Growth of the Modern West Indies. He
wrote:

In some societies the economic dependence of their
capitalist enterprises upon absentee ownership par-
alleled by their intellectual dependence upon par-
entalistic academic enterprises which are in ab-
sentia. The significance of the latter to Caribbean peoples, in terms of socio-economic oppression
and psychological poverty, is most difficult to
evaluate today. The fact that the history of each
region has been in great measure a reflection of
the struggles between rival foreign powers for the
highest profits from sugar and slaves has tended
to hide the most serious social and psychological
consequences of this situation. Nevertheless,
these consequences provide the key, in great measure, for understanding today the complexities
and problems of contemporary Caribbean society.

The emotional attachments to theological concepts from
Western Europe and North America have accelerated the social
and psychological dependence of the intellectual matrix in
Caribbean societies. Although the Caribbean people are experimenting with various ideological influences, such as
nationalism, cooperative socialism, democratic socialism,
social democracy and various local national movements, the
environment is still susceptible to rapacious forces of
intellectual exploitation and new forms of economic dehumanization.

The Caribbean person is trying to become disentangled
from these external Babylonian ideas. There are many hurdles
which are expressed very admirably by the Rev. Edmund Davis
(General Secretary of the Jamaican Council of Churches) in
his book, Roots and Blossoms.

The contemporary Caribbean person regards this
expansion as an aggressive attack on one's own way
of life. It is difficult if not impossible to ex-
tricate the Christian faith from other areas of
Western aggression. Most Christian missionaries
have assumed that European civilization and Christianity were but two sides of the package of beliefs
with which they sometimes patronized the rest of
humankind. However, West Indians think that the
Christian faith should be distinguished from its

past historical association with metropolitan political, economic and cultural aggression. The Cross
is not a symbol of European domination, but one of
forgiving love.

Evangelization and Europeanization

Unfortunately, evangelization was neither conceived as a
dynamic force to liberate people from dehumanizing social and
economic structures, nor as a revolutionary power with which
Caribbean people might change their status from dependent
beings and become co-creators once more with God, creating
possibilities for converting themselves into liberated human
beings within a concrete historical setting. Evangelization
being divorced from the political context (the community of
brotherhood/sisterhood) served the interests of the neo-colonial political, economic organizations and institutions. Using western European religious symbols, Caribbean people were
encouraged to assume the culture of western Europe. And with
this culture came a "theology of individualism." This view of
evangelical testimony saw evangelization as merely repetitive
proclamation of the Gospel, but never as a prophetic vehicle
to discern the times, in which Christ must become incarnate.

The evangelization process inherited from North America
and western Europe failed to emphasize the fact that evangelization should reflect both the diakonia (service to the
world) and koinonia (service to the community). In other
words evangelization ought to place the political culture
at the service of the liberated person who has become one
with Christ, not one which tries to domesticate and conditions the human personality to the culture of "consumerism."

In looking at this theme, Europeanization and Evangelization, we should read an excellent book written by the
Rev. Ashley Smith, of the United Church of Jamaica and Grand
Cayman. In 1973 in The Gospel, Liberation and the New Jamaica, he wrote:

To be God's instrument of liberation, the church in
Jamaica must make a clear distinction between what
is essentially the Gospel and that which is merely
the cultural and ideological wrapping in which the
Gospel has been transported from Europe and North
America to these shores. Nothing is wrong with

97

Europeans in their places, as Karl Jaspers, the famous philosopher/historian points out. The history
of humankind is not coterminous with European history. Unfortunately, in the great ages of missionary expansion the distinction was not and is still
not being made with any seriousness, between Europeanization and Evangelization. Some people still
preach as if the purpose of the Gospel were to make
all people like the people of North America and
Europe, many of whom are themselves avowed atheists,
pagans and anti-christs. The result of this confusion between Europeanization and Evangelization is
that many Jamaicans who find it necessary to reject
the archaic values of anglo-saxon culture and sub-
cultures think they must throw the Christian faith
and Christian ethics out with the values which they
are quite rightly rejecting. They confuse colonization with Evangelization because the colonizers
have so often played God and made no distinction
between what they wanted and what God required of
those who accept his Lordship.

This summary by the Rev. Ashley Smith applies not only to Jamaica but to other English speaking Caribbean territories,
where the false understanding of Evangelization has produced
serious theological problems for the Caribbean. What is
happening to the Caribbean today is that Americanization is
now being equated with Evangelization. The Rev. Clive Abduallah was critical of American Evangelists, because they
treated the New Testament in simplistic terms and so-called
Third World countries are made victims of this. The Bishop
of Trinidad and Tobago alluded that the Caribbean is being
invaded by so-called evangelists from the U.S.A. who present
a doctrine of Christ which is wrapped in the capitalistic
ethic and which is totally unrelated to the Caribbean region.
In addressing the Conference on Evangelism at the St. Augus-
tine Campus, September 8, 1975, the Bishop said, "The pretty,
pretty Jesus of Oral Roberts is not for the Third World. The
screaming,shouting Jesus who is an invention of Max Solbrekken
is not for us. The capitalist Jesus who is an invention of
Billy Graham is not for us either.
It is interesting to note that the Independent Evangel-

icals from the United States of North America have compiled a
document for the U.S. State Department, which asked the political directorate to do something positive about the theology
of liberation in the Caribbean, because it is preventing the
spread of "productive capitalism." So, it is very clear to
us in the Caribbean that the main purpose of U.S. Evangelization is to re-colonize the area in the interest of the western economic system. The main function of the U.S. evangelization is anti-communism and anti-socialism, which is not
deemed as being a political message! The Christian Church
in the British Caribbean has to free itself from the gnostic
dualism of American evangelization. If it is unable to do
this, history will not absolve the Church.

The Missionary Movement and the Nationalist Reaction

The two classic examples of the socio-political servitude
of the Church in the British Caribbean are the missionary
movement of the nineteenth century and the history of the
European churches during this period. The Rev. Clive Abduallah, Bishop of Trinidad and Tobago, on receiving his
Doctorate of Divinity (honoris Causa) from Trinity College,
Toronto, in 1971, declared that historians should give some
credit to the labors of missionaries, but should also disclose
their ambiguities. The unfortunate chronological coincidence
of Europe's colonial expansion and its missionary activity
should be recognized and critically assessed. The same coincidence is seen in the political, cultural, psychological
and economic expansion of the U.S.A. during the twentieth
century. This is said in very clear terms by Philippe Maury
in his Evangelism and Politics.

> The interests of the westernized British in the
> Caribbean, in Asia and in Africa grew naturally
> with their knowledge and experience obtained from
> imposing a westernized political domination. The
> churches concluded correctly that a missionary west-
> ern imperialism created a missionary obligation.
> Spain and Portugal reacted similarly in the six-
> teenth century during the first wave of European
> colonial expansion when the missionaries accompanied
> the 'conquistadores.' It is surprising that the
> European churches did not perceive that such a

99

coincidence of colonization and evangelization provoked suspicion, and that the missionaries inevit-
ably considered themselves to be political agents,
especially in the area and scandalous cases of missionaries who were really serving as agents for
their governments in their rivalries as world
powers.

In this connection it is not surprising that former U.S.
President Gerald Ford admitted publicly in 1976 that North
American missionaries were being used by the CIA for gathering valuable information for the State Department. The
churches in Jamaica were very fortunate that the PNP had a
dynamic political education program in 1976 which exposed
CIA church agents and the phantom religious organizations
which were operating in Jamaica. But, we notice that a new
program of missionary domination has started through the use
of U.S. cults, the Independent Evangelicals,· the Religious
Broadcasting stations in Latin America and the Caribbean and
some myopic Charismatics. The Ecumenical movement in the
Caribbean has to be very strong so as to prevent a new wave
of religious colonization from the U.S. through the so-
called Moral Majority.

Nationalist reaction against western imperialism had to
have an effect on the Caribbean Church, which interestingly
started outside the Church. R.R. Palmer, in his The Epoch
of the Democratic Revolution, Volume II, A Political History
of Europe and America (1760-1800) indicated that the happen-
ings in western civilization, especially in Europe and the U.
S.A. at the end of the eighteenth century stimulated changes
throughout the world. He described it thus:

A movement which however, different in different
countries was everywhere aimed against closed elites,
self-selecting power groups or discrimination that
no longer served any useful purpose. They were sum-
med in terms as feudalism, aristocracy and privilege
against which the idea of common citizenship in a
more centralized state, or of common membership in
a free political nation was offered as a more satis-
factory basis for the human community.

The Rev. Clive Abduallah, in his above cited address,

reiterated some of the ways in which the nationalist reaction unfolded in the Caribbean with special reference to the intellectuals, the working class and the trade union movements.

Reflecting on the Nationalist movement in the 1920's intellectual leadership in this revolution came from C. L. R. James and George Padmore, both from Trinidad and Tobago, who along with Norman Manley of Jamaica provided the major intellectual leadership of the Caribbean, while Alexander Bustamante of Jamaica was the undisputed leader in the trade union movement.

The revolution which began to usher in the nationalist reaction was started by the working class. The Bishop continued his excellent treatise by listing these events from a book Columbus to Castro, written by Dr. Eric Williams.

The revolution broke out in the years 1925-1938. Consider the chronology of these fateful years. A sugar strike in St. Kitts, 1936; a revolt against an increase of customs duties in St. Vincent, 1935; a coal strike in St. Lucia, 1935; labor disputes on the sugar plantations of British Guiana, 1935; an oil strike which became a general strike in Trinidad, 1937; a sympathetic strike in Barbados, 1937; revolt on the sugar plantations in British Guiana, 1937, an sugar strike in St. Lucia, 1937; sugar troubles in Jamaica, 1937; a dockers' strike in Jamaica, 1938. Every British Governor called for warships, marines and airplanes. The working class began to form trade unions everywhere - the Bustamante Industrial Trade Union in Jamaica, the Oilfield Workers Trade Union in Trinidad, the Manpower and Citizens Association in British Guiana...Political parties began to emerge - the nationalist movement was on the march.

The Bishop of Trinidad affirmed that while this social and political upheaval was taking place, the Church in the Caribbean in majestic fashion carried on as if nothing had happened. Many historians have attributed this behavior of the Church in this period to the fact that the local churches were carbon-copies and extensions of the churches in the metropolis,

so they could not join in revolution. Others assert that
the local churches being dependent in many ways on the western European economic system would lose their missionary
support. Although this statement is correct, yet the nationalist movements forced the Caribbean Church to have a critical look at its structures, and to make sporadic changes,
but not sufficiently far reaching to remove the theological
dichotomy that existed between evangelization and political
change of human development.

Symptoms of the Adverse Effects of the Euro-American
   Evangelization

1. The Dualism of the Protestant Ethic
    If evangelization in the Caribbean is to help erradicate
unjust economic, social, cultural and political structures,
so that the "true Caribbean person" can guide his/her own
destiny and create a just society, then we must reject every
type of dualism. We must reject the dualism which confuses
evangelization with Europeanization or Americanization. We
must reject that dualism which seeks to understand and·per-
ceive human history in two parts, one secular and the other
religious; one earthly and the other spiritual. Millenium
theology and certain reactionary religious movements retard
the rich Caribbean religious experience, reinforce the spir-
itual-material dichotomy, leads to escapism and an apolitical
theological position.

2. Reincarnation of Gnosticism
    The new theological imperialism of the Caribbean produced
a gnostic point of view. This tended to regard socialist economic models as materialistic. These models should not be
associated with the spiritual origins of evangelization, according to this gnostic tendency. In the early 1970's the
Chilean Bishops Conference rejected this gnosticism when
they said: "There is no incongruity between Christianity and
socialism in that socialism offers more hope than capitalism,
of being more fulfilled and therefore more evangelical. That
is, more like Jesus Christ, who came to liberate people from
slavery and exploitation."
    People who hold this gnostic view in the Caribbean re-
gard every form of political involvement of the Church and
clergy as satanical. It will be remembered that the early

Gnostics considered all matter to be inherently evil, and so
we are not surprised that the North American evangelicals
have resurrected the gnosticism of Marcian, which has confused
numerous Caribbean religious people.

3. Neutrality

One of the characteristics of the myopic concept of e-
vangelization in the Caribbean is based on the pietistic
views which mark certain features of the capitalist ethic.
Negative pietism contains the germ of profound neutrality,
a latent neutrality in politics, a refusal to commit evangelization to structural changes in society, no clear theological position - not willing to take the side of the poor.
It is noticeable that those who say they are neutral, always
side with the rules and not the ruled. The moment we begin
to put truth, love and justice into practice we are going
to be political. By refusing to make a political choice in
order to liberate the oppressed as the Gospel demands, we
are supporting the forces of dehumanization. Certain types
of American Protestantism which have infiltrated the Caribbean have disarmed the proletariat (urban and rural) of all
their constructive and revolutionary zeal. These ultra con-
servatives from North American preach non-involvement in politics. Nevertheless, this very act is political since its
main purpose is to prevent Caribbean societies from choosing
a political system which would change the structures of domination designed, created and supported by the western economic system.

It is very revealing that many theologians are now
teaching Marxism in universities in the United States, yet
Caribbean people are being told that they should not read
this literature which is sold in the U.S. Many Christians
in the Caribbean believe that it is not contemplation that
changes an unjust system, but the transformation of the demonic economic structures. For me, neutrality is not one of
the gifts of the Holy Spirit, but rather of Satan.

4. The Protestant Ethic

The way the Protestant ethic affected the theological
thinking in the Caribbean should be examined very seriously.
Although it has contributed to the development of western
civilization - particularly technology and certain current
political philosophies - it has also produced the diabolical

forces of "individualism" and "competition." The Protestant
ethic has strengthened the cruelly competitive nature of capitalism, preventing true and genuine ecumenism, so we are not
alarmed that the Moral Majority in the U.S. has supported the
arms race. It is only a logical outgrowth of their individualism and competition. It has reached alarming proportions,
especially in urban Jamaica, where the Protestant ethic has
been institutionalized. The Churches compete not only for
souls, but for political patronage so as to erect churches
in areas where the traditional churches can be undermined.
This ethic has helped to perpetuate conflicts of class and
race reflected in the unfortunate development of some Caribbean societies. The Protestant ethic, produced the "Victim
Theology," whereby, churches are more concerned with the hos-
pitalization of the individual than with removing the causes
of the malady or problem.

The new Caribbean Church if it is going to be true to the
Gospel of Jesus Christ, must refuse the sectarian competitive-
ness which has emerged from the Euro-American class structure,
such as parochialism assumed. Ultra conservative American
Protestantism is utilizing a very subtle strategy. It is
using the economic problems in the Caribbean to denounce the
theology of liberation and blame the indigenous political
liberation movements for the crisis. So this ethic has divided the populace and tried to divert the efforts of the
people from genuine liberation and from the neo-pentecostals,
called charismatics. One of the features of the charismatic
cult is to form a haven for the frustrated middle/upper
classes who are afraid of the politics of change. A large
section of the distorted charismatics are now the new
"spiritual imperialists" who originated in North America
and are extending the politics of religious neo-colonialism.
To contain these heretical teachings it is crucial that the
Caribbean churches embark on a dynamic Christian education
program so as to counteract the "fallen angels of the Protestant ethic."

The Caribbean Council of Churches

With the birth of the Caribbean Council of Churches
(CCC), it was thought that the paternalism of both western
Europe and North America would have been defeated, thus pro-

viding the beginnings of a dynamic Christian community, which
could develop its theological perspectives arising from the
praxis of Caribbean political culture. There have been some
positive results in many areas of the CCC, but alas certain
foreign influences have impinged on the tasks of the CCC in
the following areas:

a)Christian Action for Development in the Caribbean (CADEC)
   CADEC, the development arm of the CCC has received financial contributions from agencies in western Europe. The
Third World has been raided by foreign "Aid" and so CADEC
lost credibility because it appeared to be merely serving
the interests of trans-national corporations. I am not
suggesting that CADEC allowed this to happen, but it is
known that once foreign financial agencies are involved too
deeply in the developmental planning of strategies in the
Caribbean, there is a tendency for the donor to dictate
policy and to avoid structural changes.

b)My second criticism is that I was never too sure if CADEC
understood the dangers of "developmentalism," which would
counteract structural transformation. It was felt that there
was a feeling that "project implementation was development
en tote." Some governments of the region felt that rather
than having two competing land reform programs for food
production, there ought to be cooperation with governments.
In other words, dualism was diluting CADEC's developmental
plans. The rhetoric of development was always prominent,
but we were never sure of the institution that loaned the
money. Were these foreign friends really sympathetic with
Caribbean development? Or were they tinkering with only
cosmetic solutions and impeding serious social transformation?

c)Caribbean Contact
   Caribbean Contact has the potential for counteracting
all the reactionary theological vibrations in the region.
But it has been criticized by the right in the Caribbean
Church for not being spiritual, and it has been criticized
by the left for being too neutral. This newspaper has far
more appeal in the eastern Caribbean than in Jamaica. This
is very unfortunate because it can become a serious thought
provoking organ for communicating the new theology of evangelization, within the region. It has improved tremendously

but needs to provide relevant and indepth theological analysis
which is needed badly in the Caribbean.

One of the promising signs evident in the newspaper is
that the new editorial staff has not retreated from an "Incarnational Theology" as its base. And this continues to look
critically at the movements of the Caribbean political culture.

d) I cannot say with confidence that CCC has succeeded in breaking the old order of incipient existentialist theology, which
is used to underpin and undergird individualism and the pri-
vacy of salvation in the Caribbean. There have been attempts
to understand evangelization not only as the means whereby the
Gospel is proclaimed, but the process of liberating the whole
person within the particular historical praxis. In my opinion, the main aim of the CCC is not to yearn for neutrality,
but solidarity with the poor, the marginalized and the oppressed of the region, to which Christ has called the Church.
Theology should be inductive, not merely intellectualized
faith, but must take   risks in discerning the times for the
Caribbean people.

e) Ecumenism

For too long we have talked about ecumenism in the Caribbean, which means meeting for "week of prayer" or exchang-
ing pulpits. Very seldom has ecumenism been seen as working
together for social change. The task of the CCC should be
defined in terms of the theology of liberation and not that
of the theology of fatalism. It is heartening to hear that
there are plans to begin a new Christian education curriculum
which would use indigenous material, thus psychologically beginning to do our own theology from our own cultural roots.

What Should Be Done?

Liberating Caribbean people from economic structures of
exploitation and foreign domination is an integral part of
evangelization. This action cannot use the "theology of
death," but the theology of hope must be used to reach out
to people where they are. People must be challenged to
be children of God in their own cultural, historical, political and historical setting. "God was in Christ, reconciling
the world to Himself, not holding peoples faults against them,
and He has entrusted to us the news that they are reconciled."

This suggests that evangelization should not be deemed as consisting of narrow and sporadic programs, but as global in scope. The total liberation of all humankind in Christ must be realized in an evangelical, historical base. If evangelization is divorced from human situations, from the theology of Incarnation, then it is no longer portraying and manifesting the Gospel of Jesus Christ. "The Word became Flesh and lived among us" must be the basis for our approach to evangelization.

In the Caribbean context, I would suggest the following points for consideration:

1. A new concept of evangelization in the Caribbean must embark on a creative methodology of communication which speaks of values that are truly human. These values cannot be merely imported;

2. The churches in the Caribbean cannot begin evangelization if they are not prepared to build a new Caribbean society, and to struggle against imperialist penetration;

3. If the churches are going to be serious about evangelization, then, there has to be a critical appraisal of all theological training in the region, so that the teaching mirrors what is needed in the Caribbean;

4. There should never be any separation of liturgy and evangelization. This has been one of our weak points;

5. It is impossible to talk about evangelization if we are not prepared to be tolerant of the Marxist/Christian dialogue; and

6. There has to be a new theological oreintation in the Caribbean, which is incarnational and seeks to interpret life in the historical reality.

Finally, evangelization has to be related to the complete liberation of humankind and cannot contribute to the domestication of people. Nor can evangelization merely condition people to the old decripit values of the theological perceptions and ideas of western Europe and North America.

*   *   *

EVANGELIZATION AND POLITICS

IN THE CONTEXT OF WESTERN EUROPE

GEORGES CASALIS

Lectures on evangelization indicate that we are being
evangelized continuously, that we are listening before we
speak, that we are interrogated before permitting ourselves
to be interrogated by others, whoever we may be.

A new development in contemporary history is that the
"First World" and the "Second World" have lost initiative,
creativity and in many cases even power. As to evangelization,
the predominant ideology for centuries among reactionaries
throughout the western world has been impugned radically by
the rise of what we call the "Third World," which includes a
majority of the world's people. And the majority of these
nations are dominated nations. This impugnation includes
their struggles for liberation. Many rich theologians – that
is, secure in themselves and dominant – have been removed from
their thrones, as it is said in The Magnificat, the first revolutionary hymn of Christian tradition. Contrary to traditional theologies, the "theologies of liberation" invented
their weaknesses and their complications. By vigorously at-
tacking the positions of the wealthy, they evangelized them
prodigiously. I confess with great pleasure that even I
have been made to taste the "good savor" of the Gospels.

But a new danger has appeared, a sign that always something more is required, that the battle must always be renewed – or if you wish, that you always have to let yourself
be conquered and convinced by the Holy Spirit. Let us start
in the world of white, affluent males, as referred to by Gustavo Gutierrez, James Cone, Dorothy Sölle. European theologians and sometimes even institutions which have lost ground
have renewed themselves by repeating the words which surge up
in the suffering, the rebellion, the resistance in prisons
and in martydom. Thus there developed a kind of western bur-
lesque of the theologies of liberation, which frequently reduced itself to being nothing but a new transformation of i-
dealism, clearly false and pernicious, which pretended to be
an authentic reality, a new path for the transmission of the

Gospels.

Thus at the beginning of this presentation something particularly important must be underlined. Let us not evangelize if we are not under attack wherever we may find ourselves, by the lives and for the bitter experiences of so many brothers and sisters throughout the world. Without this confrontation we are taking risks in manifesting and carrying out the Gospels wherever we may be. To evangelize is to have simultaneously a universal consciousness, fruit of a practice with planetary dimensions. I shall speak of this again, of facing this challenge: the presentation of the Gospels in my human medium, to which I am responsible.

Thus there are two essential points here: the negation of all evangelization which does not correspond to a real commitment through our own situation, on one side, and the decisive character of practice, as a source for the understanding and the true inspiration of the Gospels. In consequence, this is the question of the coherence between life and word, and, therefore, the credibility of the one who pretends to evangelize.

Brief Analysis of the Situation in Western Europe

This analysis will be necessarily rapid and schematic, but correctly related to my topic. If I understand correctly my topic is, "What does 'to evangelize' mean under the conditions of western Europe today?"

Western Europe is characterized as living fully within the the deep crisis from which capitalism is suffering, and which is assuming dramatic proportions, affecting ideology, national sentiment, the meaning of life, etc.

Four elements of the crisis are:

1) The economic level. In France at least there are contradictions and incompatibilities between expansion, monetary stability and full employment. The imperative of capitalist firms will always be to restructure industry in order to keep it competitive in relation to international competition, that is, to produce more and to consume more at ever higher prices. This means struggling against inflation, without which there would be no disequilibrium in foreign trade and exchange. Inflation has been at about ten percent officially (9.7 in 1978). In fact it is about fifteen percent. The purchasing power of salaried poeple declines, be-

109

cause salaries have increased with "official" inflation, not
real inflation. The gravest aspect is that the present government considers this a success, but it has been obtained
only at the cost of a considerable increase in unemployment.
Unemployment is presently 6 percent in France. That is, officially 1,350,000 people of the active population are now
unemployed, compared to 1.2 percent in 1970.

The capitalist system is so constructed as to have a
"reserve force of labor" which—referring to all of western
Europe—has fourteen million unemployed and puts fifteen million more, the immigrant workers, in permanent danger. The
latter are indispensable for work which Europeans do not like
or have not learned to do. Provisions for the immediate
future foresee no change in this situation, but rather that
it will become worse.

2) The social level. The objectives and values of this
human collective are always—and today more than even—those
of convenience, those of security, those of wealth, elements
which present themselves as fundamental to the "happiness"
proposed for millions of people. Nevertheless there is a law
which knows no exception in these dynamics—that the rich are
getting richer and the relative difference between rich and
poor is growing every day. Thus in France it is officially
estimated now that the average income of the 14,000 most
wealthy taxpayers averages, officially, 50,500 francs monthly,
or $11,200. Still there are over 2,300,000 who receive on
the average 590 francs, or $125 monthly. The ratio is about
85 to 1.

This situation has no effect on the relations between
western Europe and the "Third World." Exploitation and pillage continue. There appears clearly before us a society
globally rich and dominant, its economy living on unequal
exchange with countries which are dominated, utilizing their
underpaid labor forces. Yet, it is a society which, beyond
doubt, is in a deep and permanent crisis, with social dis-
tortions and conflicts. And it is a society denying itself
in every way the possibility for making the structural changes
which are indispensable for survival. The poor and exploited
people of France who, objectively, are exploiters of "Third
World countries," voted in the majority in March, 1978, for a
systematic organization of their poverty and for the misery

of the dominated countries. Capitalism engenders its development within itself.

It seems to me impossible to interpret this phenomenon
without talking about class struggle. The forms of exploitation change, they are extremely diverse, but the reality continues fundamentally intact.

3) The political level. The explosive situation in
France of recent weeks - very violent confrontations between
demonstrating workers and peasants facing police force - is
and will be maintained by the progressive imposition of structures and principles of the Trilateral Commission. Basic here
are the concepts of "National Security" and "controlled democracy." Clearly, the different states of western Europe
are not, and surely in the near future will not be, military
dictatorships. One definition of what are called liberal
"democracies" is that "liberal democracy is the face shown
by the wealthy class when they are not afraid, and fascism
is the face they show when they are afraid." At present the
wealthy class of western Europe oscillates between triumph
and uncertainty, between hope and fear.

The ruling class has not yet reached the critical point.
Still they have set up a model state, which the parliamentary
elections of June 10, 1979, are to consolidate. This is the
social democracy of the Federal Republic of Germany, which
has several alarming tendencies. They include: permanent
ideological control, censorship and self-censorship, reductions of labor institutions - which have been converted into
mere "messengers of communication" of the patrons' power,
political discrimination against groups of Marxist politicians, a virulent anti-communism, sustenance for judical policies and generalization of the conditions for detention -
characterized by the practice of "sensory privation" (white
torture). All this must be said here too briefly, but I refer you to the works of the Third Bertrand Russell Tribunal,
of which I am a member, for more of the details of this
situation.

I experience no sadist-masochist pleasure in presenting
these ugly facts so categorically, and I would be charmed to
make comparisons with what is happening in other countries
of western Europe. Every one of the Europeans present here
should make a similar report of the dominant tendencies of his

111

or her country. Nevertheless it is obvious today that there
are really two Europes: the northern, prosperous and stable;
and the southern, economically weak and politically unstable.
Between them is France, where the dominant classes are doing
all they can to keep attached to the locomotive of the Federal
Republic of Germany, at the cost of sizable contradictions.
Thus, fundamentally, France is divided politically.

The objectives of European politics are determined by
the capitalist international and the members of the Trila-
teralism Commission who occupy its key positions. Our prime
minister is one of these, and it is interesting that the
seat of the Trilateral Commission is in Paris, in the offices
of "Electricité Francais." We can interpret from this the
activity of that institution. The objective of these politics is to put the entire continent under the domination of
the Federal Republic of Germany, with aligned governments,
by force or by conviction, this is not important. Italy,
Spain and Portugal know the conditions imposed by the social
democracy of Helmut Schmidt with the economic support necessary for making them keep permanently at a distance.

In this way the international division of labor is being
established which, bit by bit, charcterizes the German-Japa-
nese-American empire. With this international division of
labor some first line states fortify and reinforce themselves and even over-develop themselves, while the others,
in the interior of what we call the European community,
find themselves increasingly dependent. Their own economies are ever more sacrificed by the establishments and
imperatives of the transnational companies (for example,
the crisis in the French steel industry).

4) The ideological level. The present situation is
characterized by a deep "crisis of meaning" - and, from this
come the explosions of bombs and violence of the crazy terrorists, having no revolutionary meaning; and more, many
times these acts have certain counter-revolutionary effects.
Such is the case in Germany and Italy, where capitalism made
a mistake in liquidating the nazi-fascists years ago. But in
France, according to an investigation by the Commission for
Revolutionary Vigiliance, in which I participate, there were
over 40 fascist attempts in the year between May, 1977, and
May, 1978. All the various manifestations of contradictory

violence are utilized by governments – without exception – as excuses for strengthening repressive measures against all progressive forces.

On another side, the fall in the birth rate is a very interesting phenomenon, very revealing in all countries as an indication that all hope has been already lost.

To this must be added that among leftists, following the last elections in Italy and France, a wave of discontent and a spirit of demobilization has appeared which increases the generalized passivity, resignation and escapism, with reference to all political activity. This affects particularly the new groups and labor union activities. One must note that only 20 percent of French labor is organized now in unions.

The French school of "new philosophers" is the expression of the disenchantment of May, 1968. The disillusioned radical Maoist groups, above all, are spreading a philosophy of retreat to an individualism and privatism. Their three chief tenets are: 1) Marxism as a method of analysis and social change is dead; 2) All socialism leads increasingly to chaos; and 3) All human effort, particularly political effort, is imperfect, and all social change can only induce a regime worse than the present. Therefore let us maintain what now exists and not risk having something worse.

The conclusion is obvious: let us reject dreams and revolutionary mania; let us cultivate safe values – ethics, aesthetics, metaphysics. An example of this is Bernard-Henry Lévy. I would not like to give such importance to this current were it not symptomatic of a general state of apathy and if the means of communication – thus the power of transmission – had not given it great importance. The fact that the media has given it such attention is in itself revealing.

The Return to Religion

In the face of this generalized crisis of meaning, of the spirit, there is today a formidable "return to religion" which is far from innocent.

(a) The year 1976 was, not only in France but in all of Europe, the "year of Lefevre". We can only marvel at the widespread importance conceded to such a bishop, mediocre in every sense. His reactionary position shows that, in various

113

parts of Latin Europe, having a completely immobile electorate,
the only sector susceptible to revolution was, paradoxically,
that of the Christian masses. This susceptibility to revolution was shown to the extent that they have a growing preoccupation with a principle of social consciousness. Various
statistics show that militant Christians started to move to
the left in part - or, better said, among certain traditional
parishoners. In the Bishops Conference a certain progressive
current was beginning: books on the political responsibility
of Christians; opposition to the sale of arms, favoring of
economic justice and workers' rights - started circulating.
It became necessary to stop the "thaw" and Lefevre was the
instrument chosen for this purpose. His revindication as
the only representative of authentic Catholicism, his open
support of the most reactionary regimes, such as the Argentine
military dictatorship, which he held up as a model Christian
state - all this was proffered to intimidate the Episcopate
and arouse it perhaps to have no fear, in any event to taking
the position of the center-right. Thus there are great
threats in the elections which were conjured up in Italy,
France, Portugal and Spain.

In 1978 the three Popes were a great success. Paul VI,
the progressive of the "Populrum Progressario" and Medellin,
was happily replaced by the "Pope of the smile," who in turn
was miraculously relieved by a man who is young, strong, content to be Pope and, above all, is resolutely anti-communist.
Under him, without doubt, an end is to be put to all political infiltration into the Church. There have been several
indications of revindicating the values of security - such as
guarantee the true reasons for existence - from the number of
baptisms to the increased recruiting by religious orders.

(b) In western Europe we can note as paradoxical that
while "euro-communism" was apparently waning, a true "euro-
Christianity," the ideology of Trilateral Europe, was emerging. This again attests that, despite strong contradictions-
if we wish to describe a worldwide characteristic - we can
say that it is a matter essentially of a surging up of the
old idolatry of the established order: of order as established prior to and superceding everything else. The panic
induced by terror makes the churches hold themselves completely indifferent to problems of social justice, to the
demands for respect of the rights of the marginal populations

or the outcasts from society, to the struggle for the establishment of just relations with the Third World. Thus the
Board of the Evangelical Church in Germany did not hesitate
in proclaiming on September 16, 1977, after the seizure - by a
group of terrorists - of Hans Martin Schleyer, the "boss of
the bosses" of the Federal Republic of Germany, "We approve
the state we live in...only a strong state can be free."
The speech admits itself almost naturally to being anti-communist, and at the same time virulent protests arise against
aiding the movements for African liberation, despite the Program to Combat Racism of the World Council of Churches. There
are moments of protest against certain institutional positions,
such as the establishment of exceptional legislation (Anti-
Terrorist Convention); against the dangers represented by the
extension of nuclear installations or the arms traffic, which
are manifested here and there; but the system itself is never
impugned nor incriminated. The "excesses of capitalism" are
"principles" which one never incriminates. In the Ecumenical
Center of Brussels, among other places, there is announced -
in the name of historic necessities such as that of Christian
responsibility - the birth of a Europe, bastion of anti-communism, instrument chosen for the domestication of restless
peoples and unstable nations in southern Europe.

One can unhesitatingly see in this "return to religion,"
and in the importance assigned to ecclesiastical institutions,
the translation into the western European plan for the appre-
hension of religion and its utilization, such as is clearly
formulated by all the theorists of the policies of National
Security. It is a matter of giving the Christian masses the
symbols of integration into a society strictly controlled by
the transnational companies. In truth, we are seeing more
and more of what Gramsci calls "the ideological apparatus
of the state in the service of civil or repressive appara-
tuses." It is not enough, then, that the masses should be
dominated and exploited; it is necessary that they consent
to this, and that eventually they become willing to give
their lives for the defense of an order in which they themselves are the principle victims.

One must add that this takes us towards a clever dialec-
tical focus of the religious phenomenon, which is an enduring
political fact we cannot reduce only to an ideological level.
Nevertheless it is always necessary to measure the impact of

this phenomenon by economic levels. In the document "The
Church and the Powers" published in 1972 by the Protestant
Federation of France we have analyzed our ecclesiastical
reality under the triple aspect "of having, of knowing and of
being able." Ecclesiastic reality is always contradictory,
but still it does constitute itself "under pressure of real
misery" and in "protesting against this misery," particularly
in what are called the "popular forms" of religion, that is,
the forms adopted in the dominated classes.

To Evangelize

My focus is contextual, not conceptual, and my action is
correspondingly inductive. That is why it was necessary to
make this long analysis of our western European situation. If
my portrayal seems too critical, it is due to my practice of
struggling in the revolutionary party at the side of victims
of that society and in close contact with the political refugees from several military dictatorships with which France
maintains privileged relations – never vacillating in aiding
the counterrevolution – as in Zaire. And if things appear
too negative, it is because I always prefer lucidity to il-
lusions, and surprises to deceptions. I should add that
Marxist instrumentation is an indispensable theme for the
correct understanding of any reality, including, naturally,
ecclesiastic, religious and spiritual realities.

To speak of evangelization outside of a concrete analysis
of the situation is to remain on the level of myth. Still, any
analysis of a situation requires taking a socio-political position. It is not a matter of evangelizing outside of a
clear commitment of solidarity on the side of the poor; and
this raises the decisive question: Who are they, today? Who
is the historic subject of the universal future? Through whom
does the liberation actuate in our epoch? Father Marie-Domi-
nique Chenu, in a surprising statement, answers, "The human
masses – my neighbor." That is to say, following the parable
in Luke 10, "those who draw near to Me and permit Me to revive" – these are the historic subjects of today. In the
context of western Europe it means, evidently, the underpaid working masses, the millions of unemployed and the immigrant workers, the victims of radical discrimination, and
beyond all these, the masses of the "Third World," whose

116

miseries augment our enrichment. The first condition of evangelization is a class option, a commitment on the front of
anti-imperialist struggles.

Evangelization, like God, is partisan. That is, if the
Gospels carry Good News to all humankind it is not all of the
same nature. To the poor they announced the end of all exploitation, oppression and alienation; and to the wealthy,
they announce that from now on they cannot exploit, oppress
nor alienate, whoever one might be. By giving to some their
rights and denying others their privileges there results -
since their wars are opposed, some against others - a people
who are continually stumbling on their true identity: liberators and liberated. In this way the poor liberate themselves
through their own struggles, the wealthy are liberated through
the struggles of the poor. That is to say that bit by bit,
the new humanity is constituted, with blood and tears, because
class struggle and anti-imperialist combatants find no rest,
no mercy. It is necessary for Christians to learn that faith
is inseparable from militancy, and that struggle is the form
which the manifestation of liberating evangelization necessarily adopts. The eschatology is the Good News that all
this will end some day, but meanwhile we must hope: "Forward
always to victory!!"

Martin Luther King frequently said that he was struggling
in the last instance, for the liberation of the whites.
Clearly, the most pitiable victims of the ghettos, the block-
ades, the concentration camps and torture chambers are those
who make others suffer. It is for this that the Kingdom of
God comes through and by means of the class struggle, to establish classless societies; and if it be a certain fact that
the end of all forms of structural violence from which people
suffer and die will not yet be the end of history, then, yes,
this would be nevertheless a principle so new that it would
be worth while struggling for it, provided that it is within
our power to attain it, since that is our first responsibility
as human beings - or, as Aristotle said, as "political animals."

It is logical to expect that this will divide the Christian community, or better said that it will divide itself into its fundamental divisions, since the human reality and political fact in any society and in any manifestation of its
activities, whatever it might be, is contradictory to its
own self. The reality of class struggle makes such contra-

dictions oblique. Evangelization consists in not ignoring this, but on the contrary in underlining and sharpening the conditions within the bossom of the human community. In the line of the "social doctrine of the Church" or of certain clerical pretensions of the left there coincide a veritable clericalism of the left – and yet all clericalism is of the right. As Sergio Arce said in an extraordinary statement, "The poor Church – of which Vatican Council II dreamed so much – should be the free Church, since it possesses nothing – nothing but Jesus Christ." To denounce what Luther called the "Babylonian captivities" of the Church is an important part of evangelization. This criticism is as radical as loving. To be sure, politics and evangelization can engender one another, control and verify one another mutually. It is a matter here of also decolonializing the Church, that is to say, in our particular context, of "decapitalizing it."

Where does this occur in western Europe? Doubtless, rarely; still, there are numerous signs that the Gospels are producing a liberating influence and action there, also, often through isolated acts or words, like the prophets. Such is the case of Elizabeth Käseman, who in 1977 gave her life for the liberation of the Argentine people; the case of Martin Niemuller, who published an incisive article in Le Monde of May 16, 1977, "Against the Wealthy of Europe;" the case of the militant French Christians and non-Christians who are struggling to keep their lands, next to the peasants of Larzac, threatened with expulsion by an extension of a military camp. Also it is the case of communities of Christian students in western Germany who oppose the actions and conformist teaching of their churches; of numerous Italian and French clergy and laypersons who despite everything are militating in the communist and radical socialist parties; of cultural and political groups of immigrant workers; of those cooperating in the struggles of political prisoners and refugees – contrary to news reports from Europe and other places; of the struggling militants of Palestine and the Sahara; of the movement for equal rights of women and for social liberty. All these are struggling to topple capitalism in Europe, conscious that socialism can establish itself only through convergence of all revolutions. In sum, I think that in this difficult situation, which will become ever more critical, the Gospels are present, always profaning and subversive.

Now to three points which prove the reality of evangelization in our political context.

1) The intuition of Bonhoeffer in distinguishing between
religion and faith is growing daily in political importance.
It is curious that this distinction is adapting itself and is
being reactivated by the theorists of the National Security
State, but this is not by chance. The power of religion, in
its most retrograde forms - such as Lefevrian integration, or
more subtle forms like "euro-communism" - is that, above all,
Christianity is a religion of power, passion and the sancti-
fication of authority, with love of uniformity and love of
conformity. But faith, on the contrary, is the negation of
fear and of nonsense, the rejection of all ideologies, or
"crusades" and the aperture of the luminous future, despite
present risks. As Fernando Belo said, with reference to the
evangelical text, the narration is never closed, the possible
is part of reality. We are never enclosed in a box without
an exit. Doubtless faith is never without religion, but the
Gospel calls continuously for a profanation of all the glamor
and service of power and hurls itself into the conquest of
the future with all its risks, arming itself with hope. This
does not mean that we should ignore the enormous problems of
seizing and exercising power. But perhaps we cannot think
it will be very easily perverted, above all if it is a matter
of the "good power" which might be confided in persons who
really have no ambition for power?

2) Outside of the communion of sufferings and liberation
struggles, there is room for only idols, the idols of security, of triumph and domination: innumerable false gods,
whose common denominator is death, stand outside of the
struggles of the poor and exploited. The great combat of
the prophets for an exodus continues. They who serve the
living God are only they who join the long march of humankind towards liberty, when the hunger to be a people surges up
in us anew, clearly. These are the reasons why we rejoice
in being alive today.

3) All this takes us to what is truly the heart of the
New Testament, to the theology of the cross. In western
Europe, as throughout the world, evangelization is inseparable
from the high price we must pay, from the life we must offer,
from submission of will and particular interests to the great

cause of humanity moving towards the fraternal city. Evangelization is there where, very concretely, the cross is being carried, which is – as Dorothy Sölle demonstrated – a choice of class – which excludes everything, absolutely everything – the romantacism and sufferingand where the act of carrying the cross is converted into the center of the community and personal life. There one meets with victory, justice and love.

These are some of the characteristics of an evangelization which implies the radical rejection of theologies and the traditional Gospel readings. A new aspect of the Christian heritage and of ecumenical life is implied. We are speaking about counter-theologies, materialist interpretations of the Scriptures. We are passing the bread and hope in spite of all institutional barriers. We shall meet one another then in the midst of formidable tensions and enormous ruptures in all the churches, but also we shall find ourselves among living acquaintences and communions of very different people. That will be the Passover, the Easter – a new cry, an unforseen resurgence, a breach in the order of death and in the bossom of all anguishes, as in all struggle, the certainty of the birth of the new person. That is to say, we are speaking about the Resurrection.

*   *   *

EVANGELIZATION AND POLITICS:

A BLACK PERSPECTIVE

JAMES H. CONE

What is the relationship between evangelization and politics, the propagation of the faith and the building of a
just society? This is the question that defines the focus of
this essay. Unfortunately many Christians believe that there
is a sharp distinction between evangelization and politics.
They claim that evangelization refers to the preaching of the
Gospel of Jesus to unbelievers so they can through faith receive the gift of eternal life. Politics has to do with the
creation of laws that will govern people in society so that
they can live together in peace in this world. According to
this view, evangelization is the primary task of the church
with its priests, preachers and missionaries. But politics
is the job of politicians and lawyers, that is, persons who
are trained in political science and the legal status of a
given nation.

The separation of evangelization and politics is based
on the assumption that they refer to different realities.
For example, politics is limited to this world. It is a human affair that is concerned with the creation of a social
contract among people that will enhance justice and minimize
injustice. Therefore all politicians base their political
platform upon their capacity to create social structures that
will make this world a more humane place to live for everyone.

While politics is concerned with the affairs of this
world, many Christians believe that evangelization is concerned with the next world. It focuses on the salvation of
the soul, the proclamation of the Gospel to sinners, the un-
saved and the lost. Preachers, priests and missionaries,
therefore, should not concern themselves with politics because salvation has nothing to do with the material conditions of people. Their task is derived exclusively from the
kerygma of the early church, concretized in Jesus' command
to "go forth therefore and make all nations my disciples;
baptize people everywhere in the name of the Creator, the
Son and the Holy Spirit and teach them to observe all that I

121

have commanded you. And be assured, I am with you always, to the end of time" (Matthew 28:19-20). On the basis of this saying European Christians have invaded Asia, Africa and the Americas enslaving and colonizing the "pagans" so that their souls might be saved and their environment civilized. "From the beginning of the Atlantic slave trade, conversion of slaves to Christianity was viewed by the emerging nations of western Christendom as a justification for enslavement of Africans. When Portuguese caravels returned from the coast of West Africa with human booty in the fifteenth century, Gomes Eannes De Azurara, a chronicler of their achievements, observed that the 'greater benefit' belonged not to the Portuguese adventurers but to captive Africans, 'for though their bodies were now brought into some subjection, that was a small matter in comparison to their souls, which would now possess true freedom for evermore'."[1] This same "evangelistic" motive gave rise to the missionary movement during the 18th and 19th centuries and continues today to define the North American and European Chunches' involvement in the Third World.

Recently the divorce of evangelization and politics has been seriously questioned by Christians in Africa, Asia and Latin America. On each continent, there is the increasing recognition that missionaries from Europe and North America identify the Gospel of Jesus with western culture, thereby giving credence to the contention that missionary work is primarily an instrument of neo-colonial penetration. In response to the European and North American missionaries' distortion of the faith by identifying it with western culture, Third World Christians have begun to think about the Gospel in the historical context of their own struggle to liberate themselves from the relation of dependence and domination. What does it mean to preach the Gospel in the context of poverty and oppression?' And how is the Gospel related to the human struggle to create a just social order? These are some of the questions that inform the Third World perspective on evangelization and politics. In an attempt to answer these questions the All Africa Conference of Churches, in its historic Third Assembly called for a moratorium on all western missionaries,[2] and the Christian Conference of Asia and many Latin American Christians supported them.[3]

Naturally the struggle to relate evangelization and politics has necessitated a new theological approach defined

122

not by Europe and North America, but by Asia, Africa and Latin America. These theologies are shaped by the particularity of the political situation on their continent. That is
why the name of the continent rather than a particular confession of faith has been chosen as a description of their
theological starting point: African theology, Asian theology
and Latin American theology of liberation. Each theology is
characterized by its struggle against the dominance of Europe
and North America, and its creative attempt to fashion a
perspective on the Gospel that arises out of the people's
struggle to liberate themselves from oppression.

In addition to Christians in Asia, Africa and Latin America, there are also oppressed Christians in North America who
have rejected the Euro-American divorce of evangelization
from politics. They include women, Native Americans, Hispanics, Asians and Black Americans. Each of these communities recognizes the need to develop a theology out of their
historical struggle for freedom. For Black Americans, this
recognition shaped our religious consciousness. Our percep-
tion of the connection between evangelization and politics
was defined on the slave ships, the auction block and the
Underground Railroad. In the historical context of oppression and our struggle against it, we realize that the Good
News of the Gospel could only mean our political liberation
from the chains of slavery. While the white missionaries
introduced Christianity to African slaves, "the meaning
which the missionaries wished the slave to receive and the
meaning which the slave actually made were not the same."[4]
Because the reality of the freedom they encountered in the
Gospel involved its implementation in society, African slaves
found white churches socially unacceptable as a place of worship. Therefore they created their own church structures
that would more accurately represent their affirmation of
faith in their struggle for freedom. In the northern section
of the United States, Blacks created radically independent
church structures.

This independent church movement began when Richard Allen
and other Blacks walked out of St. George Methodist Church in
Philadelphia in 1787, because they refused to accommodate
themselves to segregated racial barriers erected by the white
members of that church. From this incident emerged the African Methodist Episcopal Church which was officially organized

in 1816. Later other Blacks followed suit in New York and organized the African Methodist Episcopal Zion Church in 1821. Similar events occurred among Black Baptists.

However, even Blacks who remained in white denominational structures often refused to accept the divorce between preaching the Gospel and the establishment of justice in the land. Such persons as David Walker, Nathaniel Paul and Henry Garnet are prominent examples. No one expressed this point any more clearly or more radically than Garnet. In a famous address to the slaves in 1843, he said:

> If...a band of Christians should attempt to enslave
> a race of heathen people...the God of heaven would
> smile on every effort which the injured might make
> to disenthrall themselves. Brothers and sisters,it
> is as wrong for your lordly oppressors to keep you
> in slavery as it was for the one thief to steal our
> ancestors from the coast of Africa. You should
> therefore use the same manner of resistance as would
> have been just in our ancestors when the bloody foot-
> prints of the first remorseless soul-theif were
> placed upon the shores of our country...Liberty is
> a spirit sent from God and, like its great Author,
> is no respecter of persons.[5]

For Garnet, evangelization was not only preaching in words but also the undertaking of action to release and to liberate. This is the ethos that shaped the Black churches' involvement in the abolition of slavery.

African slaves' refusal to separate evangelization and politics forced them to create an invisible institution in the South, because it was illegal for them to assemble without the presence of a white person to proctor the meeting. Therefore African slaves organized secret worship services in the slave cabins and woods at night in order to fashion a perspective on evangelization that transcended white interpretation of the Gospel. Carey Davenport, a former slave, remembered those meetings: "Sometimes the cullud folks go down in dugouts and hollows and hold they own service and they used to sing songs what come a-gushing from the heart."[6] Another ex-slave from Texas, Adeline Cunningham, made a similar report: "No suh, we never goes to church. Times we sneaks in the woods and prays de Lawd to make us free and times one

of the slaves got happy and made a noise dat they heered at
de big house and den de overseer come and whip us 'cause we
prayed de Lawd to set us free."[7]

Unlike white missionaries and preachers who identified
evangelization with the proclamation of the Gospel to unbelievers and heathens, African slaves identified it with the
proclamation of freedom. That was why they sang:

Oh Freedom! Oh Freedom!
Oh Freedom! I love thee!
And before I'll be a slave,
I'll be buried in my grave,
And go home to my Lord and be free.

Other slave songs such as "Go Down Moses," "Steal Away"
and "Oh Mary, don't you Weep" express the same liberation
theme. This theme not only defined the rise of the Black
church in the 18th and 19th centuries but continues today to
give political direction to the Black church's involvement in
Black people's struggle for justice. The refusal to divorce
evangelization from politics is the chief reason why the
Black struggle for justice has taken place primarily in the
church. As most of the slave insurrections were organized in
the Black church and were led by preachers, also the contemporary movement of Black liberation in the 1950's and 1960's
took place in the context of the proclamation of the Gospel
in the Black church. Martin Luther King, Jr., is an international symbol of a pervasive reality in the Black Christian
community.

It is within the context of the Black church's participation in Black people's struggle for political justice that
Black theology's origin must be understood. Black theology
was not created in seminaries and universities but on the
streets of Harlem and Watts and in the context of the rise
of Black Power, as Black people attempted to fashion a political project consistent with their knowledge of themselves
as creative, free human beings. When Willie Ricks sounded
the cry of Black Power during the James Meredith March in
Mississippi (1966), it was a clarion for Black people to
take charge of their history. Once again we Blacks realized
that if we are to be free, we must ourselves create the revolutionary structures for the implementation of that freedom.
Expecting white oppressors to participate in the creation of

political structures that will liberate us is like expecting
Pharoah in Egypt to respond affirmatively to God's demand to
"let my people go!"

The contemporary appearance of Black theology happened
as Black people attempted to give theological structure to a
political commitment they had already made. Black theology
became the theological arm of Black Power by defining Black
people's political struggle as identical with the Gospel of
Jesus. The title of my first book in 1969 reflects this
political stance, Black Theology and Black Power.[8] My second
book followed a year later (1970). It introduced liberation
as the central motif of the Gospel which[9] is reflected in the
title, A Black Theology of Liberation. Since the publication
of these two books, other Black theologians have supported me
in joining the Gospel with political struggle, even though
they have not always agreed with the way I have done it.
They include, J. Deotis Roberts,[10] Major Jones,[11] Gayraud S.
Wilmore,[12] and Cecil Cone.[13]

White North American theologians' response to Black theology has been interesting but consistent with their usual
failure to take seriously Black people's struggle for freedom. Often without even reading the literature on the subject, some say that Black theology is nothing but racism in
reverse. Others, still refusing to emerge themselves in the
social history out of which Black theology comes, get sophisticated and clever in their reply by accusing Black theologians of reducing Christianity to a political ideology and
thereby failing to recognize revelation as the starting point
of the Gospel. But the great majority of white theologians,
who feel uncomfortable remaining silent on the theme of liberation, ignore Black theology by dealing exclusively with
Latin American liberation theology. These theologians turn
liberation theology into a new theological fad, a commodity
in that what they say about Latin America does not necessarily require of them a revolutionary act in their own social
context. Much of their talk remains in the seminaries and
universities, and it often appears that all that is necessary
to demonstrate their commitment to the poor is to write a
book about them or to attend a conference on the subject.

Although Union Theological Seminary in New York has done
far more than any other North American white seminary for
Black liberation, yet it is an excellent model of the danger

126

about which I speak. For example, we have many white lib-
eration-oriented professors and students, but their pre-oc-
cupation is primarily with Latin American liberation theology.
And there are many courses on that subject in the Union cata-
logue. Also students and professors take field trips to Latin
America, and Union presently is trying to establish a structural relationship with seminaries on that continent. Now I
am not against all this, because I firmly believe that we need
a global perspective in theology. But as I have said to my
Union colleagues, there is no way, absolutely no way, for
them to demonstrate a real solidarity with the poor in Latin
America without taking sides with poor people in North America. Union is located on the edge of Harlem, the largest and
perhaps the most oppressed Black community in the U.S.A., but
it is difficult to get Union Seminary faculty and students as
a community to make a political commitment in solidarity with
Black people in that community. I have raised this concern
many times but their reply is that Black people have many able
spokespersons. But my reply is: So do Latin Americans! The
issue is not whether Blacks, Latins or Africans have able
spokespersons but whether we have genuine allies in the
North American white community.

   After much reflection, I have come to the conclusion that
most of the North American whites who talk about liberation
theology do only that, namely, talk and nothing more. For
the only way that I can know that any person means more than
talk is for him or her to make a political decision for poor
people in their own historical context. And I know what decision you have made by the company you keep, by whom you
regard as your friends. And essentially, whites still remain
exclusively within the framework of their own racial group.
Whatever we say about class, which I firmly believe is central
and perhaps the primary contradiction, yet I do not believe
that the race problem in North America or the world will be
solved by focussing exclusively on the economic problem. I
know that many white North Americans use the class issue as
a way of ignoring their own racism.

   However, I am very much pleased to say that there are a
few white theologians who have taken the time to read, listen
and participate with an openness to encounter the truth inherent in the Black struggle, and I have found dialogue with
them enriching and creative. When I meet white persons who

want to dialogue not because of guilt or some other con-
descending motive, but because their own humanity is at
stake in Black people's struggle, then I know that I have a
genuine dialogical situation in which much mutual learning is
possible.

While this genuine mutuality is hard to find among white
persons in North America and Europe, such is not the case in
Asia, Africa and Latin America. I have sought to deepen and
to enlarge the political focus of Black theology by entering
into dialogue with theologians who have a Third World consciousness. That is why I gladly accepted the invitation to
come to this conference in Cuba. It is also why I have attended similar conferences in Asia, Africa, Latin America
and the Caribbean. My experiences on these continents have
disclosed more clearly the global context of oppression, and
I feel compelled to reflect that reality in my theological
project.

The Black Theology Conference in Atlanta, August, 1977,
may be dated as the beginning of Black theologians' attempts
to take seriously the international context of oppression.
This global perspective is found not only in my lecture entitled "Black Theology and the Black Church: Where Do We Go
From Here?"[14], but more importantly in the "Message to the
Black Church and Community"[15] that was written as the official statement of the conference. Since the Atlanta meeting,
I have attended conferences in Mexico,[16] Ghana,[17] and Sri
Lanka,[18] each of which focussed on ways that Third World
theologians can meaningfully share a common theological project that will be beneficial in the struggles of oppressed
peoples from which we come.

Presently I am in Cuba, and I am hopeful that our being
together will contribute to a further clarification of the
theological task, so that we can return to our respective
communities with a clearer vision of our responsibility in
the struggle for freedom. It is within the context of dialogue and in my belief that we have much to learn from each
other that motivates me to say a further word about evangelization and politics. I want to examine briefly 1) evangelization and salvation; 2) evangelization and politics; and
3) salvation and eschatology.

I. Evangelization and Salvation

If we are to understand correctly the relation between
evangelization and politics, I believe that it is necessary
to state clearly the content of salvation we have been entrusted to proclaim. How can we evangelize if we do not know
what salvation means? Without a clear perspective on salvation, we will remain confused about whether politics has anything to do with preaching the Gospel.

The place to begin is with the Bible. In the Old Testament, salvation is grounded in history and is identical with
God's righteousness to deliver people from bondage. Literally
the root meaning of the word salvation is "to be wide or spa-
cious, to develop without hinderance, and thus ultimately to
have victory in battle."[19] The Savior is the one who has
power to gain victory, and the saved are the oppressed who
have been set free. For Israel, it is Yahweh who is the
Savior because "the Lord saved Israel that day from the hand
of the Egyptians; and Israel saw the Egyptians dead upon the
seashore" (Exodus 14:30). That is why the people sang:

> The Lord is my strength and my song,
> and He has become my salvation;
> This is my God, and I will exalt God,
> The Lord is one of war;
> The Lord is God's name.   (Exodus 15:2-3).

Here salvation is God's deliverance of the people from political danger. It is God's divine righteousness to liberate
the weak and the oppressed. Salvation therefore is an historical event of rescue, and event of freedom.

There are several terms which describe God's saving activity, and they include deliverance, redemption and healing.
Almost without exception, in the Old Testament, the Deliverer,
Redeemer and Healer is God. And the delivered, the redeemed
and the healed are oppressed people. It is impossible to understand the Old Testament view of salvation without recognizing it is God's deliverance of helpless victims from physical suffering or political menace.

In the New Testament, the Old Testament emphasis on God
as the One who effects salvation, and salvation as historical
liberation is not denied but reinforced and carried through
to its most radical consequences. In the New Testament as

in the Old, God is the Savior par excellence, and God's salvation is the revolutionary historical liberation for the oppressed of the land. That is why it is reported that Jesus
was born in a stable in Bethlehem, and why Mary describes the
divine meaning of Jesus' coming presence with these words:

My soul magnifies the Lord,
and my spirit rejoices in God my Savior.
For...the Lord has shown strength with God's arm,
God has scattered the proud in the
    imagination of their hearts,
God has put down the mighty from their thrones,
    and exalted those of low degree;
God has filled the hungry with good things
    and the rich God has sent empty away.   (Luke 1:47+).

The identification of salvation with freedom from bondage
in history is revealed in the New Testament through Jesus'
identity with the poor. He came to and for the poor; he ate
with the outcasts, the "bad characters" of his day, the ones
whom the Pharisees called sinners. He healed the sick, be-
stowed the blind their sight, and restored health to the lame
and the crippled. When John sent his disciples to Jesus asking "Are you He who is to come, or shall we look for another?"
Jesus replied, "Go and tell John what you have seen and heard:
the blind receive their sight, the lame walk, lepers are
cleansed, and the deaf hear, the dead are raised up, the
poor have good news preached to them." (Luke 7:20+). These
acts locate salvation in history, the concreteness of human
existence. If the Kingdom of God (God's rule) is identical
with Jesus' person, and if his person is inseparable from
his work, then there is little doubt what salvation means.
It is the bringing of wholeness and health in the conditions
of brokenness, peace and justice where oppression exists. In
a word, it is the restoration of people to their true humanity. Salvation is the bestowal of freedom for the unfree,
redemption for the slave, acquittal for the convicted and
deliverance for the captives.

As people who have encountered this event of liberation
in Jesus Christ, the Church has been called into being to
spread the Good News of salvation to all humankind. The
Church's task is to be the embodiment of salvation that it
has encountered in Jesus' death and resurrection. Evangelism

therefore, arises from a natural ingredient inherent in the Church's being. For if the Church does not spread salvation, it denies the one who makes into identity as a Christian community possible. Therefore it is not evangelistic for any selfish reason of its own but because of a theological necessity that arises from its own identity in Jesus Christ. Because all people belong to Him, through the salvation He has wrought for them, the Church excludes itself from that salvation if it tries to possess it as a property of its own. It is out of this Biblical understanding of salvation as liberation that we must understand the relationship between evangelism and politics.

II. Evangelization and Politics

Because salvation is grounded in history, there is no way to separate the preaching of the Gospel from a political commitment on behalf of the oppressed of the land. If there is no salvation independent of the struggle for liberation in history, independent of the emancipation of people from the chains of slavery, then there can be no Christian proclamation apart from the political commitment to fight against injustice, slavery and oppression. Evangelization, then, is not only the proclamation of thoughts about freedom found in the Bible or in my head. Rather it is primarily participation in the socio-historical movement of a people from oppression to liberation. Anything less than a political commitment that expresses one's solidarity with the poor in the struggle for freedom is not Christian evangelization. For the word Christian connects evangelization with politics and thus requires that the one who dares to claim that identity must necessarily make a historical commitment identical with the struggle of the poor for freedom.

When Christians recognize the demands that their faith places upon them, they then begin the search for tools that will help them actualize it in society. It is because faith does not have within its own confession the social tools necessary for its implementation that we are required to look elsewhere. If evangelization is inseparably connected with the political demand to liberate the poor, what resources do we need in order to accomplish that task? It is at this point that we realize that justification by faith alone is not

131

enough. In order for the poor to experience a justification
in which the Lutheran emphasis on the forensic declaration is
transformed into liberating social structures, then faith
must connect itself with a social theory of change. How can
the poor liberate themselves if they do not know why they
exist in poverty? How can the oppressed free themselves from
bondage if they do not understand the world that enslaves
them? It is because Latin American theologians take seriously
the structures of economic oppression that they have turned
to Marx as the primary resource for their liberation theolgy.
Black theologians have similar resources for an analysis of
racism. The same is true for feminist theologians in relation to sexism. Anyone who claims that evangelization
is connected with politics but ignores the need to develop
a social theory of change does not intend to be taken seriously.

However, liberation theologians, whether Black, Latin,
African or feminist, need to stay in constant dialogue with
each other lest they become too narrow in their approach to
liberation. We need each other because there can be no genuine freedom for anyone until all are free. If we do not
remain open to each other, then we will simply negate the
truth not only as it arises out of another social context
but also as we have encountered it in our own. For Blacks
to ignore class oppression or sexism simply turns the Black
struggle into a male middle class preoccupation, without any
real change in the capitalistic structures that oppress us
all. But a similar middle class and racist emphasis is
possible among Marxists and women. The only way we can help
to protect ourselves from this fallacy is that the persons in
our struggle represent the revolutionary consciousness reflected in the complexity of our historical situation.
Therefore Blacks, women and poor persons, who have a revolutionary consciousness, must be present as we attempt to create a social theory of change. For without their presence,
there is no way to guarantee that their unique interests
defined by their color, sex and class, will play a significant role in shaping the social structures of the new, revolutionary society.

III. Salvation and Eschatology

Although evangelization is connected with politics because the Biblical view of salvation is grounded in history,

yet we must not fail to say a concluding word about an even
more radical dimension of the New Testament view of salvation.
The radical character of the New Testament view of salvation
is not its rejection of history. To reject history in salvation leads to passivity and makes religion the opiate of the
people. The New Testament, while accepting history, does not
limit salvation to history. As long as people are bound to
history, they are bound to law and thus death. If death is
the ultimate power and life has no future beyond this world,
then the rulers of the state who control the military are in
the place of God. They have the future in their hands, and
the oppressed can be made to obey the law of injustice. But
if the oppressed, while living in history, can see beyond it,
if they can visualize an eschatological future beyond this
world, then the "sigh of oppressed creature," to use Marx's
phrase, can become a revolutionary cry of rebellion against
the established order. It is this revolutionary cry that is
granted in the resurrection of Jesus. Salvation then is not
simply freedom in history; it is freedom to affirm that future
beyond history. Indeed, because we know that death has been
conquered, we are truly free to be human in history, knowing
that we have a "home over yonder."

"The home over yonder," vividly and artistically described in the slave songs, is the gift of salvation granted
in the resurrection of Jesus. If this "otherness" in salvation is not taken with utmost seriousness, then there is no
way to be sustained in the struggles against injustice. The
oppressed will get tired and also afraid of the risks of freedom. They will say as the Israelites said to Moses when they
found themselves between Pharoah's army and the Red Sea, "Is
it because there are no graves in Egypt that you have taken us
away to die in the wilderness? What have you done to us, in
bringing us out of Egypt?" (Exodus 14:11). The fear of freedom and the risks contained in struggle are an ever present
reality. But the "otherness" of salvation, its transcendence
beyond history, introduces a factor that makes a difference.
The difference is not that we are taken out of history while
living on earth - that would be an opium. Rather it is a difference that plants our being firmly in history because we
know that death is not the goal of history. The transcendence-
factor in salvation helps us to realize that our fight for
justice is God's fight too; and God's presence in Jesus'

resurrection has already defined what the ultimate outcome will be. It was this knowledge that enabled Black slaves to live in history and not to be defeated by their limitations in history. To be sure, they sang about the fear of "sinking down" and the dread of being a "motherless child." They encountered trouble and the agony of being alone where "I couldn't hear nobody pray." They encountered death and expressed it in song:

> Soon one mornin', death comes a creepin' in my room.
> O my Lawd, O my Lawd, what shall I do?

Death was a terrible reality for Black slaves and it visited the slave quarters leaving orphans behind.

> Death done been here, took my mother an' gone,
> O my Lawd, what shall I do?
> Death done been here, left me a motherless child,
> O my Lawd, what shall I do?

In these songs are expressed the harsh realities of history and the deep sense of dread at the very thought of death. But because the slaves knew or believed that death had been conquered in Jesus' resurrection, they could also transcend death and interpret salvation as a heavenly, eschatological reality. That is why they also sang:

> You needn't mind my dying,
> Jesus' goin' to make up my dying bed.
> In my room I know,
> Somebody is going to cry,
> All I ask you to do for me,
> Just close my dying eyes.

NOTES

1. Albert J. Raboteau, Slave Religion: The Invisible Institution in the Antebellum South (New York, 1978). p.96.

2. For a report on the May 12-24, 1974, Lusaka Assembly, see The Struggle Continues, All Africa Conference of Churches, Nairobi, Kenya, 1975.

3. See _International Review of Mission_, a special issue on "Moratorium," Volume LXIV, No. 254, April, 1975. For a response of the Christian Conference of Asia, see "Let My People Go" by Harvey Perkins, Harry Daniel and Asal Simandjuntak in _Mission Trends No. 3: Third World Theologies_, eds., Gerald H. Anderson and Thomas F. Stransky, C.S.P. (New York, 1976).

4. Raboteau, _Slave Religion_, p. 126.

5. Henry H. Garnet, _An Address to the Slaves of the United States of America_ (New York, 1969) p. 93.

6. Cited in George P. Rawick, _From Sundown to Sunup_, (Connecticut, 1972), p. 40.

7. _Ibid._, p. 35.

8. (New York, Seabury Press, 1969).

9. (Philadelphia, Lippincott, 1970). My other books are _The Spirituals and the Blues_ (New York, 1972) and _God of the Oppressed_ (New York, 1975).

10. _Liberation and Reconciliation: A Black Theology_ (Philadelphia, 1974).

11. _Black Awareness: A Theology of Hope_ (Nashville, 1971) and _Christian Ethics for Black Theology_ (Nashville, 1974).

12. _Black Religion and Black Radicalism_ (Philadelphia, 1972).

13. _The Identity Crisis in Black Theology_ (Nashville, 1975).

14. See _Cross Currents_, Vol. XXVII, No. 2, Summer 1977.

15. See _Ibid._

16. This was a conference called primarily by Latin American theologians in Mexico City, October 7-10, 1977.

17. See _African Theology en Route_.

18. See _Asia's Search for Humanity_.

19. F.J. Taylor "Salvation" in Alan Richardson (ed.), _A Theological Word Book of the Bible_ (New York, 1960), p.219.

*   *   *

EVANGELIZATION AND POLITICS:

A NORTH AMERICAN VIEW

ROBERT MCAFEE BROWN

How are we to relate the two words of our theme? My
task is first to report on some ways this is being done in
North America from a white perspective and then to offer
some reflections of my own on what I see happening. What
follows is an attempt to share with a wider audience some of
our quandaries and dilemmas.

A Report

1. While most Christian groups on an official level
would acknowledge some relationship between evangelization
and politics, their actual institutional life probably denies
their words. When all is said and done, they would really
mean that the choice is evangelization or politics. Both are
part of life, but the Christian cannot really do both, and
perhaps should not do both. So a first way of answering the
question becomes evangelization, period. Let the church
stick to its true task, which is saving souls and not stoop
to "horizontalism" or "activism" or "reduce" the Gospel to a
technique for human relations.

We are all familiar with this position and need not lin-
ger over it, save for the following comments. a) it does not
avoid politics, but simply ignores the fact that its disengagement is really a vote for engagement on the side of the
status quo; b) it frequently does take political positions,
i.e. when its own right to speak or evangelize is being questioned, or when there is a "clear mandate" from the Gospel,
such as the self-evident truth (to proponents of this position) that Christians must "fight communism" by whatever
means are necessary in order to "maintain the American way
of life;" c) we should perhaps let such people alone, since
when they do enter the political arena, it is invariably with
the far right-wing. But let us be forewarned: this is a
rapidly growing point of view.

2. A somewhat more refined position would argue for a chronological treatment of the topic: evangelization, then politics. This can be expressed in several ways: a) the first and basic task is to convert individuals so that their lives are transformed; then those transformed individuals can work to transform society through individual involvement in political structures; b) evangelization is an individual matter, politics is a social matter, and the only proper order is from the individual to the social, not the other way around.

We have all confronted this position, too, and we discover that if we take it seriously, we can never in one lifetime move from the first stage to the second, since there are always more people who have not yet been evangelized, and even by the end of our lifetime, those who have been evangelized will also die, and there will be a whole new generation to be evangelized before political engagement can begin. In actuality, the shift from evangelization to politics can almost always be successfully postponed.

On a more refined level, this position can be raised to a theological principle: we must first work out a "theology of politics," after which we can "apply" it, i.e. first Gospel then politics. This implies that the "principles of the Gospel," are developed in a vacuum (i.e., a theological seminary or a professor's study) and possess a truth quite independent of their expression in human struggle. A questionable assumption...

3. A model widely practiced seeks to have it both ways: evangelization is the church's collective task, whereas politics is the Christian's individual task. This position seeks to be very open. "Of course" its proponents will argue, "individual Christians should engage in politics. That is their personal responsibility to society. The church must encourage them to do so. But since there is no clear 'Christian position' on complex political issues, on which all Christians can agree, the church itself should refrain from 'taking sides.' Furthermore, if the church collectively takes a stand, that will divide those members of the church who do not agree with the collective decision. They will be alienated; the church will lose its ability to minister to them; there will be discord and alienation where there should be harmony and reconciliation."

Those who adopt this position (and they are many) are willing to tolerate a certain number of mavericks within their midst as the price to be paid for avoiding collective stands by denominations, so long as the mavericks behave decently and do not become too numerous.

By easy extension, the argument that "the church should stay out of politics" becomes "ministers and priests should also stay out of politics." Let them train the laity in theological or ethical or moral principles, but when it is time to head for the streets (or even the polling booth), let the minister stay in the manse, the priest in the rectory and remain unspotted from the world. The pope's first speech at the Bishops Conference in Puebla will give comfort to such an extension of the argument.

Once again, the proponents of the position fail to realize that: a) inaction is a form of action, since neutrality is impossible and supports whoever has power at the moment; b) a church that can separate collective and individual responsibility so easily is fostering a defective understanding of church; c) a position that understands reconciliation as disengagement from the possibility of conflict misses the point that reconciliation is appropriate only after, and not before, genuine conflicts have been unmasked that need to be faced rather than avoided; d) a view of ministry that limits it to cerebral activity rather than engagement, and suggests that ordination divests one of the right to personal political involvement, is equally suspect; e) those who mount the argument need to be challenged as to their consistency, since they do not object when the church implicitly supports the right, but only when it explicity moves a shade to the left.

4. We are seeing the rise of another position in North America: evangelization is politics of a particular sort. The Gospel becomes effectively equated with how its exemplars stand on a single issue. The clearest example is found in some (though by no means all) quarters of American Roman Catholicism, where the characteristics of the true believer is to be militantly against abortion. One may pass lightly over other articles of the faith, so long as the eleventh commandment is strictly adhered to: Thou shall not abort an unborn child, nor shalt thou allow anybody else to do so either."

The context of the issue can change: Protestants had a similar position on prohibition a generation ago, and surely in the sixties there were those for whom being against the war in Viet Nam was the _sine qua non_ of responsible Christian witness.

The danger here is not just fanaticism, which may in itself be a species of Christian virtue, but ugly fanaticism which expresses itself in bombing abortion clinics, ceaseless harrassment of women who enter them for counselling, simplistic versions of moral truth ("Anyone who counsels abortion is a murderer") and so on. As this position is clarified, it is interesting to discover that "single issues" people become locked into a pattern where both their modes of action and their convictions on other issues soon become predictible with a high degree of accuracy.

5. Each of the above positions is visibly present on the North American scene (along with many others that could be mentioned). Is there another position that could move beyond some of the shortcomings? Let me briefly describe a new position that is only beginning to emerge. While it has learned from Latin America and other parts of the world, it is trying self-consciously to deal with North American realities. It could be described as from politics to evangelization to politics to evangelization to...in such a way that the two are never finally separable. People within the group known as "Theology in the Americas" (which grew out of the 1975 Detroit Conference) are trying to put this into effect through various interest groups that are struggling to find a new way to "do theology" in the midst of engagement. I will not try to make extravagant claims for what is being accomplished, but state only that an attempt is being made to face the issues. A variety of constituencies are attempting to do this – women, Hispanics, Blacks, Asian-Americans, Native Americans, even "professional theologians." Concerns surface out of the particular situations and struggles in which such people live and work; these are reflected upon together in the light of whatever faith people bring to the situation or have refined out of the situation, and the situation can again be entered in the light of the new reflection, after which...and so on.

To the charge that such efforts are divisive when done by many separate interest groups, it can only be replied that this is acknowledged, but is a price presently being paid for the self-awareness and search for self-identity that each

group needs. A conference in summer 1980 ("a second Detroit")
is being planned to see if by that time some coalition can
emerge that can unite the separate groups around some commonly
shared agendas.[1]

Some Reflections on the Report

Out of this spectrum of responses to the question of the
relationship of evangelization and politics, what issues
emerge that call for further reflection? Here is a sampling:

1. The variety of ways, both implicit and explicit, in
which evangelization and politics are separated from one another, suggests the need for further reflection on both terms.
Evangelization is frequently understood in individual or pri-
vatistic or moralistic terms; it is forgotten that the whole
person is involved, that the "evangel" or Good News must
speak to bodily as well as psychic concerns, that there is an
irreducible political dimension to evangelistic concern, or
the message is not being communicated in all its fullness.
Conversely, there is an "evangelical" dimension to politics,
reflected in a politic that likewise speaks to the whole person and is not trying to divide the human being into a dual-
istic construct, i.e. spirit/body, or whatever term one
chooses.

2. A sustained criticism of most North American efforts
would have to focus on our deficient understanding of evil.
We fail to see what can be called systemic evil, evil as em-
bodied in social structures that almost defy our attempts
to transform – or destroy – them. The popular view that it is
enough to "change individuals" apart from efforts to change
the social structures that entrap them, is foredoomed to
failure because it does not measure with sufficient seriousness the evil inherent in the very structures themselves.

To diminish the pervasiveness of that evil will require
different instruments of measurement than we have previously
employed, and heightened degrees of engagement in struggles
we have consistently avoided. There is needed not just a new
"understanding" of evil and its power, but a willingness to
do battle with it precisely as an expression of our political
evangelical task. This will mean challenges to our political
and economic system of a magnitude we have not yet attempted
and for which we do not yet have the tools.

3. This implies new efforts to cope with the meaning of power in our situation. Whereas most people in the world have to cope with having too little power and must find ways to get it, our problem is having too much power and being unwilling, if not unable, to relinquish it. It is clear (at least to me) that if we do not find ways to begin to share power, both domestically and internationally, it will sooner or later (and probably sooner) begin to be taken from us. Here is an evangelical-political problem of the first order: how can power be shared creatively rather than hoarded destructively? How can we create alliances toward this end with people who have no reason to trust us and every reason to distrust us (Blacks, Chicanos and many others)? How can the competing agendas of various special-interest groups be so adjusted that they can work together on enough common agendas to make trouble for "the principalities and powers of this world"?

4. Is it really possible to work effectively within the churches, considering the degree to which the churches have been co-opted by the system, and derive benefits from the very structures of society that act so destructively upon others? Is it not unrealistic to expect institutions (even - or especially - Christian institutions) to deny the very groups that legitimate and support them in the social structure?

On the other hand, is it possible to "use" institutional structures for ends other than they intend, "exploiting" them in creative ways to support social change rather than the status quo? And if we leave these structures, where, we must ask wistfully, are we to go?

A Spectrum of Political Options

In the light of such considerations, let us outline some of the political options open to white Christians in North America, who are trying to keep evangelization and politics closely tied together. Here I confess to considerable bafflement, and hope for wisdom from those who have had to face similar problems in their own situations.

A spectrum of possibilities:

1. To exercise one's political concerns through either of the major parties, seems increasingly futile (with one possible exception I will discuss later). One is increasingly

141

co-opted into support of structures and principles that are at most palliatives, designed not to impact the system. About the most one can do by voting Democratic is to keep Republicans out of office. The price to be paid by doing this, however, is very high, namely putting Democrats in those offices since the distinguishing characteristics of the two parties are increasingly difficult to discern.[2]

2. In the light of such baleful choices, a classic response had been to opt for a third party. But this means twenty years of ground work during which unending damage can be done by the incumbents, whether Republican or Democratic. At best, such a party could hardly build a constituency large enough to be more than a "balance of power" between Republicans and Democrats, a rather unexciting choice (see above).

A word should be added for the benefit of Latin Americans who see this strategy as one they have already rejected, i.e. tercerismo, seeking a third way, an option that always ends up, when things get tough, in support of the right rather than the left. The North American choices, however, are of a different order: they represent not a choice between the right and the left, but between the right and the far right. In this case, creating a third party might mean, over the long haul, creating a second option.

3. If it should ever occur to white Christians to follow a European model and create a Christian political party, the thought should be suppressed as rapidly and as permanently as possible. Such a party would be reactionary to the core, and possibly provide a gateway to fascism.

4. The paucity of creative choices leads some Christians to despair of ever doing anything through politics, save using it as a device to see that things do not get too much worse — which is certainly beneficial to those who will be victimized if things do get worse. Perhaps there is a role for those, who, not hoping for too much, try to continue to play the role of creative gadfly, riding herd on the policies of all government agencies and officials.

The danger here is that prophets who operate without a power base are not usually taken very seriously by those in power; they may even be honored. They can surely be tolerated in the name of what Marcuse has called "repressive tolerance."

If the stance of creative gadfly were part of the long range plan to create a third party, however, it might have greater strategic attractiveness.

5.   There is another possibility: trying to create a socialist wing within the Democratic party. This has the merit of not starting from point zero, but of taking advantage of an already existing structure and of dealing with at least a few people initially who may be won over to one's cause. The difficulty of course is that the Democratic party has powerful interests that will work long and well to avoid anything resembling a "socialist takeover." However, should they be sufficiently threatened to initiate a purge, that action alone could create the nucleus for a third party.

The above options do not exactly leave one gasping for joy. To the degree that all of them fail, Christians may be left with the necessity of creating some alternative sectarian model of as self-sufficient a kind of community as possible, simply to provide small alternatives in the present that could prefigure long-range hopes for the future. But I do not yet know how one would go about this.

Interlude: What Do We Have Going For Us?

The possibilities for creative relationship between evangelization and politics in North America seem rather dismal. Yet there is one sociological factor that may offer creative possibilities to white Christians and if so, we should be aware of it and use it. This is the reality in the United States of a pluralistic culture. Despite all efforts to the contrary, it has not yet been possible to impose a single intellectual, cultural or religious mind set on our nation. There is, up to a point, elbow room or "breathing" space for a great variety of points of view. I do not want to be naive about this, or claim for it more than I should – particularly as far as militant minority groups are concerned – and the oppressive and physically destructive treatment of such groups as the Black Panther Party (in the area of the country where I was living at the time) is a reminder of the limits to this pluralistic toleration.

But as long as there is any space for alternative socio-economic-religious positions, that space should be claimed and guarded and used. It is possible, in other words, for small groups representing new positions to find ways to survive and begin to grow. Exxon will not initially be worried by a collective exploring alternative economic models and a network of such groups across the country could begin to take shape.

The other side of the picture, of course, is that as such groups do take shape and present even minimal threat, they will face challenges often very subtle and therefore the more powerful, to their ongoing existence, from Exxon and everybody else. But the ability to organize at all is itself an important reality, not to be ignored in the present except by those who believe that the shape of the future is foreordained beyond the possibility of challenge.

To speak a dissenting work, let alone do a dissenting deed, in most Latin American countries today, is to court death, and no one from elsewhere is entitled to decide that someone else should become a martyr. At present, however, for white Christians in North America to speak a dissenting word or do a dissenting deed is to court disapproval and perhaps some personal inconvenience, but little else. Consequently, in a world where political conformity is more and more imposed by force, we should make more rigorous use of whatever degree of initiative our own pluralistic situation still allows.

Are There Some Special Tasks for the Churches?

While I am not hopeful about denominational structures moving either far or fast, I do feel that there may be "remnants" within them where some creative experiments could take place. Perhaps we can learn some things from the experience of the comunidades de base in Latin America. Let me indicate three sample issues:

1. White churches need to face the challenge of making themselves, their facilities and their resources available to the voiceless in our North American society and elsewhere, so that the voiceless can begin to speak for themselves. This is something very different from being a "voice for the voiceless," which involves a paternalistic speaking for, or on behalf of someone else, rather than letting those who need to speak do so for themselves. The way in which the National Council of Churches became the vehicle which the Amer-

ican Christian Community had to listen to the "Open Letter to North American Christians" sent from a group of Central American Protestants before our 1976 election, is only a small example of what I have in mind. This letter was a hard-hitting attack on U.S. policies of domination in Latin America, suggesting the need for us to lean heavily on our own power structures at home if we are going to combat the "silent genocide" far from home. (I have a strong suspicion that most of the document was written on the very campus in Matanzas where we are meeting).

2. Coupled with the need to provide a platform for the voiceless, is the need for the churches (or a remnant within the churches) to insist on our seeing ourselves from a global perspective. I do not know of any other place within our society where this can even begin to happen, and it is a perspective essential to our national life and use of power, for it affects the destinies of a large portion of the global family. The church at least claims to be a part of, and exemplify, the global family, and this means the necessity of thinking and acting from global rather than national or class or racial interests as our primary concerns. I see an increasingly gloomy scenario for the future unless this can begin to happen.

This is not a matter of concentrating on what is happening far away, in order to ignore what is going on at home. Two considerations are important here: a) much of what is going on far away is our responsibility as the "Open Letter" reminds us, so that our focus has to shift back to the power structures here at home that act repressively; and b) we are forced to confront the fact that the very things that are happening abroad are happening at home – racial indignity is two blocks away as well as two continents; and economic exploitation of Hispanics happens in the central valley of California as well as in the poblaciones of Santiago, Chile. To "think globally" therefore, is not to concentrate just on the distant scene, but to realize that the distant scene and the scene near at hand are one and the same. Each can sensitize us toward that part of the whole that we want to ignore. I continue to hope that a remnant in the church might be the initially frail and feeble agency through which some of this could begin to happen.

3. Another task for North American white Christians, and one that is not going to be popular, is to begin to confront the issue of our affluence in relation to the rest of the world (as well as the rest of North American society). Sister Marie Augusta Neal, a Roman Catholic sociologist, is one of the few people I know who has even posed the question, let alone tried to provide a response. She asks, "If the Gospel to the poor is the message of liberation and the recognition that they have the right to rise up and claim what is rightfully theirs, what, then is the Gospel for the non-poor?" And she answers her question by suggesting that the Gospel for the non-poor must be a Gospel of diminishment, one of relinquishment, of "letting go."

By this she means much more than simplified life-styles of the individual, which may conscienticize the individuals who adopt them (though they may also prematurely suggest that such actions have solved the problem), but which can easily be co-opted by the establishment in such a way that nothing whatever has changed. Sr. Marie Augusta means basically that on a national scale we must begin to find ways of sharing power, taking practical steps to release others from our enslaving power (moratoria on international debt payments owed to us, for example) to which could be added drastic reductions in armaments expenditures, both in what we manufacture for ourselves and what we sell to others.

Such proposals are not, as our saying goes, "going to fly in Dubuque," i.e., they will not draw widespread support among grassroots constituencies. But until we realize that the world is not for much longer going to let the rich grow richer while the poor grow pooer, and that inordinate concentration of wealth in the hands of the few is going to be an increasing liability to those few as world opinion comes to focus against them, we are living with our heads in the sand.

Conclusion

From one perspective, I imagine that I should end this report on a penitential, even breast-beating, note. That North America is a prime contributor to global and domestic oppression is patent, and the fact that white Christians are complicit in these realities is also patent. How can white

North American Christians confront Chileans or Nicaraguans or
Vietnamese or Black North Americans or Chicanos or whoever -
without a sense of shame and guilt?

However, it is increasingly my experience that the so-
called "white American guilt trip" is finally immobilizing.
We do not act productively out of guilt (if we act at all).
We simply end up acting on our own behalf, instead of the
neighbor. If acknowledgement of guilt is the beginning of the
journey, it is not the end. I think our biggest problem is
not our explicit belief in the all-pervasiveness of guilt,
but rather our implicit belief in the all-sufficiency of
rhetoric.

Some of us are learning a new way of looking at the
world; we have discovered new tools of social analysis. We
know more clearly who the enemy is. We engage in a "re-read-
ing of the Scriptures." We can even pronounce the word "conscientization" without stumbling.

But for so many of us that is the end of the road, or
almost the end of the road. Our real problem is not to gain
new insight, it is to move from insight to deed. We "do
theology," which Gustavo Gutierrez calls "the second act"
without having engaged sufficiently in what he calls "the
first act," which is commitment and a very specific kind of
commitment: commitment to the poor.

We are, in other words, disturbingly like the Rich Young
Ruler, in his disturbing encounter with Jesus - an episode
that every single exegete I have ever read in the northern
hemisphere manages to tame and domesticate so that it is de-
fused of real challenge. We are going to have to ask - and
answer - what it could mean, politically and personally, for
us to sell what we have, give to the poor, and for the first
time, follow Jesus.

Perhaps for us that is the question above all others in
which evangelization (our own evangelization, this time) and
politics are so joined that they can never truly be separated
again.

NOTES

1. Since the above essay was written, Detroit II has been held and did signal the development of some coalitions, particularly among Christian so-called minorities. cf.

2. Since this essay was written we have been vested with a new administration whose policy of "Reaganomics" is rapidly destroying fifty years of legislation on behalf of the poor. Some differences are re-emerging.

*   *   *

CLOSING REMARKS

SERGIO ARCE MARTINEZ

Beloved Sisters, Brothers, Friends, Comrades:

On this occasion, being called on to close these meetings, my final words are those of gratitude – gratitude to God, then to each one of you, including our non-Christian comrades who have attended this event so zealously, as we all have, contributing their energies, their interests and their enthusiasms.

These meetings have meant to us – to the Evangelical Seminary of Matanzas and to the Latin American and Caribbean Christian Peace Conference – a heartwarming dream of gathering together in this socialist, revolutionary country, the most representative of the theological currents which are fully committed to the people, to the poor, to the Church and to the society of the future.

If there have been any positive results at all, I should say they might be summarized as follows:

First, we have found common grounds for understanding one another, on the points which were noted at the beginning of the meetings – lying beyond our pluralism and diversities in an evangelical commitment which involves the political, liberating mediation of the doctrine of Jesus Christ. It is interesting to note that in one way or another, perhaps without wishing for it, we have been able to identify that the evangelizing politics of the Gospels in countless cases are coincident with the politics of socialism.

Second, I think we have achieved a sense of community which is broader than ever on our theological duties. This has cost us labor, effort and occasional misunderstanding, but having come from diverse parts of the earth we have agreed that action in a praxis of liberation well integrated with the people – the masses – is essential for evangelization. We have created, it seems to me, a climate of mutual confidence for continuing our labors for all humankind – I should say, of community labors as a matter of conscience for a Christian people committed to the liberation struggle of all people.

Third, all the points, the weak points, which once bound

149

us to a certain idealistic subjectivity - I am thinking of the Latin American theologians who chattered vaguely during the discussions of principles ten years ago in the early movement of Christians for Socialism - these points have been made more realistic. Today we are more objective in gathering up all the experiences of the early years on our continent.

Fourth, I believe we have assimilated the messages from Oaxtepec and Puebla, and, perhaps, advanced beyond them in developing the points which are essential for genuine evangelization, not only for our own people but for the world.

The agonies of the Vietnamese from the beginning of their wars have moved us all. Viet Nam continues to be a symbol of perseverance in struggle, of unlimited heroism; and we have known how to condemn here the aggressors, clearly and thoroughly.

We have remembered Ernesto Cardenal who sent us fraternal greetings and who told me he regretted deeply being unable to be with us, due to his responsibilities in the evangelical and political struggle. We have remembered him and his Nicaragua. We have remembered our African friends of the Frente, and our suffering friends in Puerto Rico.

Many of you have not been to Cuba previously, but I think we have all been enlightened by the realities of a socialist Cuba, with the only socialism existing in the New World. Hugo Assmann says it need not be sought on a planet lost somewhere in the skies, but Cuba is a socialism located in history, with all its weaknesses, with many aspects still awaiting change. But it is the only one we know in the New World and one for which us Cubans is a reality that cannot be turned back.

Together with our brothers and sisters from the socialist countries of the east and our North American brothers and sisters, who mean so much to us; with our brothers and sisters in the rest of Latin America, Asia, Africa; together with all these brothers and sisters we have made a just judgement of the role being played by the theology of liberation today. And there is one sign of hope which has been translated into reality. I think we have discarded a great deal of sectarianism, of euphuism. We have spoken in Jesus' name and sought together a common pathway, fortifying the unity which will save the Church. The Church will be saved whenever it makes itself one with the people. The destiny of the poor,

we have said, is the destiny of the Church. Despite everything, in these meetings we have witnessed and we have proved
that the sign of hope has become reality, since we have
recognized that our common destiny is the Kingdom.

The prophetic and evangelizing voice has been sounded
as much for the countries of the east as for those of the west,
of the periphery as for the center. This is truly the result
of a genuine ecumenism which, it seems to me, has characterized this meeting.

On the other hand I wish to refer to what I said at the
beginning. I recalled the name of Camilo Torres. Here is
his picture. Following his advice, if you wish to put it
that way, we accomplished - at least the organizers accomplished - this event. Perhaps among the list of those in
attendance his name should have been included, because Camilo
is, indisputedly, the model Christian of this century, exem-
plifying for us the pathway for the fullest and most committed participation by Christians in the creation of a better
world. That Christian participation which he propounded was
primarily one with a theoretical basis of commitment with a
double perspective: one he called theological, the other,
scientific. He described them thus: "The position of Christians should not oppose, but should enhance the well-being
of humanity." This is what Camilo meant by the "scientific
perspective." He added, "If this good, this well-being, cannot be realized without changing the present structure of
society, it would be sinful for Christians to oppose such
change." This for Camilo was the theological perspective.

For Camilo this Christian participation implied, furthermore a political tactic of unity over any sectarian interest.
This tactic too he considered from a double perspective, one
general and one specific. He described them as follows to a
group of Christian students, "Integration with the masses is
essential for the revolution and for unity. These are not
our patrimony; they belong to the workers and peasants. They
will be the ones to guide us, to make demands of us; the ones
who forge our unity, over the heads of bossy caudillo person-
alities."

This analysis of Camilo has primary importance for
Christian leaders throughout the world, particularly for each
one of us here. Camilo continued his analysis of unity, saying, "We favor all revolutionaries, wherever they come from,

and we oppose all anti-revolutionaries, wherever they come
from. We will not be split by religious differences, not by
ecclesiastical differences. Today, unfortunately, the Church
of Jesus, the carpenter's son - who, as Luke said, has no place
to lay His head but on a stone - His Church, unfortunately, is
a Church visibly prostituted by the rich. But the gravest
problem of the Church is not having priests who use their
ministry to increase their own personal economic well being;
not so much that as the situations of having profitable properties owned by religious communities and the institution,
which nevertheless do not permit management by the ecclesiastical hierarchy but by those who conserve and preserve the
properties - in other words, Church properties managed by
people with a capitalist mentality."

"We see that those hierarchies who rule the Church have
a completely conformist mentality and are subjects of the
oligarchy, therefore we understand that Christianity has been
falsified, that it presents itself to the people, as the
Marxists say, 'as opium for the people.' Therefore we are
not going to let ourselves be divided, as has been attempted
many times, by anguishing national problems. Why should communists and Catholics discuss whether God exists or not when
both are convinced that misery exists? Why do we sit in
cafes discussing whether the soul is mortal or immortal when
we all know that misery is mortal? We will not let ourselves
be deceived by these discussions; let us go to the roots for
benefiting the populace. Let us make a campaign. Let us do
what will make us be judged to be Christians: to provide food,
housing, clothing, education. By these acts shall we be
judged. No one will care whether or not we are wearing little
medals, or are praying to this or that saint. We believe
that Christ lives within each of our neighbors, whether communist or Protestant, and especially that Christ lives in
each of the poor. For whatever we do for the poor we do for
Christ."

Finally for Camilo, Christian participation in the building of a just world included a political strategy with a single orientation or perspective which he expressed in very
clear, concrete terms. "It is indisputable," he said, "that
we will advance to socialist structures of society." Referring to this he said in a press interview, "A true Christian
should collaborate with all those revolutionaries who propose

to change the present unjust and oppressive social structures. It is that change which characterizes the world of today: what is now happening in Colombia is part of that change. What is determining it is pressure from below, as much here as in Viet Nam. Therefore the American intervention in Viet Nam, which is a veritable crime, will fail; however many guns they use or however many people they kill. They will be beaten. Yes, I say - as I said in 1965 - Christians ought to take a definite position, as such, in that struggle. Christians, if they wish to be really such, not in words alone, ought to participate actively in such changes. Passive faith is not enough for communion with God; active love and charity are essential. This means, concretely, living in the human fraternity. And today it means living in the peoples' revolution, in the necessity for joining 'the weak and oppressed nations, for ending all exploitation, and standing by them rather than by the oppressors'."

That is why I said earlier that our meeting is held under the advice of Camilo, because the thesis of Camilo of Christian participation in the construction of a better world remains, perhaps, better expressed in his own words than by any others, speaking from a west European background; and I want to emphasize this so that no one would wish to give an incorrect interpretation to Camilo's thinking, nor a false airtight interpretation. He said, "Socialism can be built without destroying the essentials which exist in Christianity."

For us - and I am speaking as a Cuban Christian - this is a living reality, as it is for our brother and sister Christians from other socialist countries. Would that each one of us might have his/her own similar experience soon! But I shall add something more: our experience of socialist, Marxist-Leninist revolution in our country makes us rephrase Camilo's statement a bit, without changing its meaning. It is not only that socialism can be built without destroying the essentails which exist in Christianity. It is, that we know through our own experience - and this is the testimony with which we wish to end these meetings: we know because of the living revolution of these twenty years, because of the reality of this new Cuba, the better Cuba we are building, that only by the construction of socialism, by a socialist world, will it be possible to save the essentials which exist in Christianity.

*   *   *

MESSAGES

Message To Dr. Kurt Waldheim, Secretary General, United Nations, New York.

We, 78 Christian theologians from Europe, Asia and Latin America, the Caribbean and the United States of America, assembled at the International Meeting of Theologians, called by the Evangelical Seminary of Theology of Matanzas, Cuba, and the Latin American and Caribbean Christian Peace Conference; condemn the aggression of the People's Republic of China against the people of Viet Nam. We demand the complete withdrawal of Chinese troops from Vietnamese soil, and we urge that the Security Council do everything possible for the restoration of peace and justice.

International Meeting of Theologians, Matanzas, Cuba.
February 25 - March 2, 1979.

Message to the Christians of Viet Nam

To:

Committee for Patriotic Catholic Liason, Hanoi.
Mons. Nguyen Van Binh
   180 Phan Dinh Phung
   Ho Chi Minh City
Christian Council of Churches

A group of Christians from Europe, Africa, Asia, Latin America and the Caribbean and the United States of America, lovers of peace who struggle against imperialism and all forms of reactionary oppression, have gathered together at the International Meeting of Theologians under the title "Evangelization and Politics." The brothers and sisters attending this event now taking place in Cuba, called by the Latin American and Caribbean Christian Peace Conference, and the Evangelical Seminary of Theology of Matanzas, feel it to be their unavoidable duty to communicate with you, Vietnamese Christians, to express to you our spiritual unity during the tragic experience of your people during the invasion by the government of the Peoples' Republic of China.

The political preservation of the liberty and independence of Viet Nam constitutes the indispensible condition and the essence of evangelization for you. In this struggle, at this time, please receive and accept the admiration, the esteem and the community in Jesus Christ from us Christians from various parts of the world. We make the words of the Evangelist as ours, of weeping with those who weep and of suffering with those who struggle, furthermore, of struggling with those who struggle and of encouraging those who are seeking liberation. Oh brothers and sisters, Vietnamese Christians, you are not alone; the God of peace and justice is protecting you, and you may be certain that many Christian lovers of peace throughout the world are standing with you at this time of trial for your people.

Through you we wish to express our solidarity with the Vietnamese people in their struggle against the government of the Peoples' Republic of China. We are certain that once more the people of Viet Nam will know how to overcome their difficulties, and that victory will shine forth eventually.

- Matanzas, Cuba.

STATEMENTS AND DECLARATIONS

Statement on Nicaragua

We, theologians and leaders of Christian churches in Europe, Africa, Asia, the United States of America and Latin America and the Caribbean, 78 in number, now assembled at the International Meeting of Theologians in the Evangelical Seminary of Matanzas, Cuba, and the Latin American and Caribbean Christian Peace Conference cannot fail to express our firm solidarity with the Nicaraguan people, led by the heroic Sandinista Front for National Liberation, against the dictatorship of Somoza, one of the oldest tyranies known on the American continent or the entire world.

We realize that in Nicaragua forces of opposition to Somoza have been organized which, in one part, should give room for maneuvering to a national bourgeoisie with a form of "Somozism without Somoza," that is to say, without fundamental changes in the economic structure of the country; and in another part, a force for approaching and unifying sectors with a project which is solidifying the formation of a Patriotic Anti-Somozist Front. Within this range of possibilities we manifest our broadest solidarity with the Movement of the United People (MPU), which has maintained the firmest and most consistent positions for the liberation aspirations of the Nicaraguan people, because we know that from this Movement there can arise the popular government of broadest national unity, overcoming the Somozist military dictatorship and dismanteling the praetorian National Guard.

We believe in the power and the patriotism of the Nicaraguan people and that the only solution of its national problem is the above named organization of the people.

We salute and endorse the patriotic unity of the Nicaraguans.

To a Nicaraguan People freed from Somoza and the stigma of Somoza!

International Meeting of Theologians, Matanzas, Cuba.
February 25 - March 2, 1979.

Statement on Viet Nam

We, theologians of Christian churches in Europe, Africa, Asia, Latin America and the Caribbean and Latin America, and the United States of America, numbering 78, now assembled at the International Meeting of Theologians called by the Evangelical Seminary of Theology of Matanzas, Cuba, and the Latin American and Caribbean Christian Peace Conference, cannot refrain from declaring ourselves opposed to the aggression of the government of the Peoples' Republic of China against your valiant country, the heroic people of Viet Nam.

We realize that the irresponsible invasion by the government of China into your country has seriously endangered peace, justice and stability in the world. This aggression represents the greatest degree of betrayal of an historic project, in open retrocession which has converted itself into an instrument of world reaction, that it is an act of aggression against a new society which is rising up victorious after a long and cruel trial of struggle. As witnesses of justice and peace of God for humankind and for the world, we cannot remain quiet in the face of unjust acts which threaten world peace. We raise our voice together with all those who proclaim the right of Viet Nam to build a better future for itself.

We all feel under great historic debt to your small but important people. Your struggle, launched against French colonialism and North American imperialism, has left indelible impressions on the history of humankind. Our solidarity with your people at this time is our solemn duty. Thus we unite our voices, indignant, to demand the complete withdrawal of China from Vietnamese territory. We proclaim the right of Viet Nam to reconstruct its society in peace and with liberty. We would consider ourselves guilty before God and history if we remained silent in the face of the prepotent attitude of the Chinese government.

May your people receive our expression of solidarity against the aggression of the government of China, and our hopes and convictions that you will emerge newly victorious so that justice and peace may enlighten humanity.

International Meeting of Theologians, Matanzas, Cuba.
February 25 - March 2, 1979.

162

Statement on Mozambique

> Co. Samora Moises Machel
> President
> Popular Republic of Mozambique

We, 78 theologians of Christian churches in Europe, Asia, Africa, Latin America and the Caribbean and the United States of America, now assembled at the International meeting of Theologians called by the Evangelical Seminary of Matanzas and the Latin American and Caribbean Christian Peace Conference, cannot refrain from speaking out against the aggressions of the illegal government of the Britsh colony of Southern Rhodesia against your country and the heroic people of Mozambique and the people of the Front Line Countries.

We are aware that the increased aggression - in number and in degree of violence - against your country and your people, in recent days, cannot be disassociated from the irresponsible aggression of the government of the Popular Republic of China against the valiant people of Viet Nam. We cannot allow ourselves to be deceived by the imperialist manuever of diverting world attention from your struggle, in distracting the international solidarity which has always been positively with the people of Zimbabwe and the people of the Front Line Countries. We are certain that it is not a matter of an isolated act, but that it is a desperate and hopeless action of imperialism against the countries which have decided to construct a new society, after their long struggles against oppression and domination.

At this time we express our solidarity with your people, as a part of our duty, and we also reaffirm our solidarity with the people of Viet Nam and with all peoples in struggle.

We unite our indignant voices for the immediate cessation of aggression by Rhodesia against the Front Line Countries, and we recognize the right of the people of Zimbabwe for complete and immediate independence.

We would consider ourselves guilty before God and history if we were to remain silent at this time.

We request that you transmit to your people, and to the presidents of the Front Line Countries, this expression of our solidarity, our hope and our conviction that your people will be victorious, so that justice and peace may shine on humanity.   - Matanzas, Cuba.

Statement on Vieques, Puerto Rico

A group of theologians of Christian churches from Europe, Africa, Asia, Latin America and the Caribbean and the United States of America, 78 persons called together by the Evangelical Seminary of Theology of Matanzas and the Latin American and Caribbean Christian Peace Conference, at the International Meeting of Theologians in the city of Matanzas, Cuba, now express:

1. Our denunciation of the serious situation on Vieques, an island municipality of Puerto Rico. The United States Navy is presently occupying three quarters of the area of Vieques, and because of its continuous naval exercises – naval and aviation practices in marksmanship, similated disembarcations, experimenting with new arms, etc. – is impeding the activities of the inhabitants of Vieques in their fundamental rights to productive labor, to their tranquility and, in general, to a full and happy human life. In economic terms, it is frustrating the development of the island in agriculture and fishing.

2. We are concerned that world peace is endangered by the naval maneuvers and the bellicose utilization of the island by the armed navy of the United States. The bellicose naval complex which the United States maintains on Vieques and the eastern part of Puerto Rico constitutes the principal threat to world peace in all Latin America. Furthermore, Vieques is used for naval exercises by other countries of NATO and other allies of the United States.

3. We affirm our solidarity in the struggle of the fishermen of Vieques, the population of Vieques and of Puerto Rico in general, favoring the soonest departure of the bellicose United States Navy from Vieques.

International Meeting of Theologians, Matanzas, Cuba.
February 25 – March 2, 1979.

FINAL DOCUMENT

FINAL DOCUMENT

Seventy eight Christian theologians from churches in Africa, Asia, Europe, Latin America and the Caribbean and the United States of America, invited by the Evangelical Theological Seminary in Matanzas and the Latin American and Caribbean Christian Peace Conference, met together from February 25 through March 2, 1979, at the Seminary in Matanzas, Cuba. Our theme for reflection and discussion was "Evangelization and Politics."

The Meeting was marked by an atmosphere of frankness, of unrestrained criticism and of community which permitted full confrontation among the varied points of view and positions. Also we felt ourselves stimulated by the happy spirit which one senses in Cuba during the construction of a socialist society.

The atmosphere of seeking unity in the attainment of solidarity with the poor in their struggle for liberation, marked this dimension of Christian ecumenism: we found ourselves united with Christ in the liberation of the oppressed.

Two important recent Christian events were reference points during the Meeting: the Assembly of Protestant churches of Latin America held in September, 1978, in Oaxtepec, and the Third General Latin American Bishops Conference held in early 1979 in Puebla.

We were glad to see how the rediscovery of the fundamental evangelical option of the liberation of the poor served to unite us and free us from many of the confessional barriers which had raised walls of separation between us. As it was said in Oaxtepec, "the historic subject of the unity of Christians with the people are the poor of Yahweh to whom Jesus Christ announced their liberation through His death and resurrection." (Pre-informe No. 2, Role of the Church in Latin America, I.5).

We were stimulated to deepen our commitment to the poor and the dispossessed by the Declaration of Puebla. "The evangelization of the poor by Jesus was one of the Messianic signs, and for us too it will be a sign of evangelical authority." (No. 896). "Human promotion, in its aspects of development and liberation is an integral part of evangelization." (No. 247).

Our faith in Jesus Christ teaches us that we are evangelized, and we now evangelize through whatever means we are
capable of, in truth and by our works, demonstrating that the
poor and the meek are blessed forever, because they possess
the earth (Psalm 37:8-9, Matthew 5:3-4). Evangelization for
us must center on truly carrying on, in the name of Christ,
this struggle so that the poor and dispossessed may gain,
some day soon, their inheritance of the earth. They are the
subjects of this process: "The historic overcoming and dis-
placement of the reigning structures of power will come from
an organized populace which designs and carries on its struggle by means of new, distinct means." (Oaxtepec, Op. cit.
I,10).

Today the dispossessed are especially that immense number of people in the dependent and underdeveloped periphery
of Asia, Africa, Latin America and Oceania. Because of the
hopes and the plight of these people, and because of their
struggle to make out of themselves a power sufficiently for-
ceful to let them share in the evangelical promise of in-
heriting the earth, we have developed these days of theological reflection. In the light of the contributions of the
social sciences we have deepened "through prayer and spiritual discernment" (Puebla, Introduction) the significance
of the relationship between Evangelization and Politics, between the poor and their liberators, through the constitution
of a suitable power.

The presence at this Meeting of theologians from Europe
and the United States follows the universal character of
evangelization. Christians have been united through all time
by the prayer of Jesus for the coming of the Kingdom, in
which we affirm the eschatological and eternal horizons of
our hopes. We believe that in the current socio-political
situation, the signs of the Kingdom will be demonstrated concretely in the struggle of the poor to be liberated.

The specific theme of the meetings was Christian reflection on politics. In this area we shall make some contributions, which neither negate nor undervalue other central
aspects of the good news of Jesus Christ for the poor.

If Puebla "encourages the knowing and denouncing of the
mechanisms which generate this poverty" (No. 925), and if it
"Unites its forces with those of other churches and of people
of good will for uprooting that poverty and making a more just

168

and human world" (No. 926), then we find ourselves in this
union of forces and in the task of clarifying our tasks.
With this introduction, let us offer some reflections from
these recent days.

The Biblical Meaning of Poverty

As Christians we cannot begin to understand the massive
misery of the times – especially in the peripheries – without
seeking help from the Bible.

In Latin America the new reality of the Church in solidarity with the oppressed sends us to the Bible. But this
makes us interpret it from a position of solidarity with the
poor. In times past the prevalent interpretation of Bible
readings – with some exceptions – was one of seeking a place
for the Church in a world which produced misery. We now need
a fresh, communal and popular interpretation of the Sacred
Scriptures, in order to engender faith in a new world.

Our interpretation of Biblical readings centers on the
observation of the privileged position given to the poor,
seen particularly in two areas – the exodus from Egypt and
the teachings of Jesus. In the first, God commanded Moses
to free the slaves from their oppressors (Exodus 3:7-10). In
the second, Jesus announces, mediating powerful acts, the
Kingdom of Heaven for those possessed by evil spirits,
the blind, the dumb, lepers, prostitutes and the hungry
(Matthew 11:2-6; Acts 10:38).

In order to describe precisely this privileged position
of the poor and avoid demobilizing interpretations, let us
indicate that God is not impartial in the confrontation of
social classes. God demonstrates justice in favor of the or-
phan, the widow and the stranger as they face their exploiters (Exodus 22:20-23; Deut.10:16-19). The Bible mentions
the power of the poor, saying that the God of gods is with
them. In this affirmation of the power of the poor we note
a clear coincidence with revolutionary theory.

The evangelical story describes the presence and power
of God on the side of the poor precisely as solidarity with
them. (We find a synthesis of this idea in Corinthians II:
8-9: "For you know the grace of our Lord Jesus Christ, that
though Jesus was rich, yet for your sake became poor, so
that by His poverty you might become rich.") This corrects
the interpretation which saw the God of Exodus as benefactor
of the poor from a position outside of history, an interpre-

tation which leads us today to the well known problems of paternalism. According to the evangelical story, God walks with the poor in order to emerge out of poverty with them.

The evangelical story tells us that God walking with the poor is an act of combat, since the poor are being exploited and have enemies who deny them their power (and with it the powerful presence of God). Through our daily experience we can see that class struggle is real and we can see that it is the exploiters who start the struggle. In this situation it should not be surprising that solidarity with the poor must assume the class struggle. In the New Testament we read that Jesus and His disciples fought with demons and priests, and even with the pious and paternalistic Pharisees.

Under these conditions to accept the Good News of God means converting ourselves – a conversion to God and to a solidarity with the exploited in their struggle. Now, there are those who protest, saying, "Isn't the New Testament for all people? Isn't the love of God universal?" To these we reply, "Yes, as an invitation to conversion. The rich without their paternalism will have to take their chances with the exploited as the Son of God did. The poor, for their part, will have to convert themselves away from their dreams for bettering themselves without their brothers and sisters, and affirm their participation with the people who are struggling and walking with God towards the Kingdom."

In saying that God is with the exploited in their struggles, we are announcing our faith that the decisive power of history is the power of the people ("The foolishness of God is wiser than people and the weakness of God is stronger than people." I Corinthians 25). This cannot be a triumphal faith. "No, in all these things we are more than conquerors." Better, God's struggle with us means that together we shall make our analyses, together we shall plan our strategies and together we shall struggle in the faith which princes and principalities will not be able to overcome, since God is with us (Romans 8:31-39).

Today the Periphery Evangelizes the People

Within our societies, the poor and the oppressed are the indigenous, the peasants, the workers in industries and the service sector, the collective victims of racial and sexual discrimination, the under-employed and the marginals.

But all these are found in societies which have been under international domination for centuries. Underdeveloped countries are dominated by different forms of capitalism. Their domination ought to be understood in this light.

Recent decades have seen a growing consciousness of the situation and ties between oppressed people have been strengthened. Africans have said that we are left with only one "terrible option:" liberty at any price.

Only in the negation of humanity created by capitalist imperialism are the terrible sins, which are hidden by opulence, made visible. Only in the poor is it possible to witness the negation of God which is entailed in the negation of our brothers and sisters, who are surrounded by the wealth created by their very exploitation. Thus the dominated countries on the periphery of the Empire have become the Evangelists for the countries of the Imperial center.

Some of the people of Africa, Asia and Latin America today are enriching the universal context of nations like a peripheral belt, stretching itself to unite them in a single project of emancipation. The particularities of each continent and country should not divide, but rather should strengthen— in terms of race, culture and history – the single struggle of oppressed populations.

Paradoxically, the periphery is now coming back not only as the protagonist of its own historic project, but also as a challenger of the centers of world power and of Christian duty in these centers.

The exploited themselves – designated to be privileged – are joined by those people who now appreciate the social meaning of the Gospels, liberating themselves from the captivity and manipulation to which the powerful had confined them. And they are now the exploited who, organized in small communities or larger units, are planning and projecting against these countries the liberating power of the original message of the Gospels. The poor and the exploited are showing that when the poor start living the Gospels in all their radicalness, the Gospels necessarily become dangerous and subversive for the powers of domination.

Right now the poor in all countries of the periphery are confronting, questioning and denouncing the churches of the center, their accommodativeness and their power. These Christians are announcing a future of authentic liberty for all

171

humankind. This Christian experience. is shared by all those
Christians who, in the powerful countries of the center, join
in solidarity with the periphery in experiencing the same oppression and in entering the same quest for liberty.

In countries of the center, authentic new experiences of
faith in solidarity with the periphery have emerged. Evangelization is soliciting these objectives: denunciation of the
economy of exploitation which subject people in underdeveloped countries to capitalism; solidarity actions with refugees and with political and economic exiles; contribution to
a worldwide public opinion against dictators; boycott against
transnational corporations which exploit countries of the periphery; the struggle against attempts to revive the cold war
and widening of the arms race; efforts to eradicate racism
and sexism. These and other actions in the developed countries, favoring disarmament, peace and justice for the oppressed, are further examples of how Christians carry on
evangelical tasks throughout public life. In the same way
these struggles have broad possibilities of transforming
and converting the very life of the Church.

Evangelization: Racism and Sexism

Oppression and domination are also found in racism and
sexism. Both are expressions of superiority, with corresponding inferiority attributed to the other race or sex. In
America, where the present Meeting is being held, millions
of Afro-Americans, Native Americans and Latinos - especially
in the United States - are suffering from socio-economic exploitation. This exploitation is intensified by discrimination caused by racial and sexual prejudice. At Puebla it was
noted that "indigenous and Afro-Americans live marginally and
in sub-human conditions - they may be considered the poor of
the poor." (No. 20).

At the beginning and the base of racial discrimination
and subordination lies economic exploitation. The slaves
were brought to America as captive workers. The slave trade
was a primary source for capital accumulation and slave labor
was the basis for the plantation economy.

The conquest and submission of the indigenous were rather
similar and are still occurring today among the Asians, Chicanos, Puerto Ricans and other Latinos in the United States.
Similar conditions are found in other continents also, for

172

example among the foreign workers in the richer parts of western Europe.

Discrimination against women is one of the most widespread forms of human domination. It is found in all societies but particularly in the most plundered classes - "having their condition doubly oppressed and marginalizad," as was said at Puebla (No. 898). Thus women are subject to all the more exploitation for being considered especially cheap labor. Woman under economic necessity and obligated by family poverty are exploited sexually as prostitutes. Due to our "machismo" cultural background, women are frequently made mere objects of sexual pleasure. Or they are decorative as instruments for capitalist advertisements and consumerism. Nevertheless they are often denied entry into professions and occupations for which they may be suited as individuals.

The building of a new society would be profoundly inhuman without the presence and contribution of women with equal opportunities.

Every type of exploitation requires its legitimation, its rationalization. Thus racial and sexual prejudice by oppressors have elaborate ideologies to falsify our consciences and maintain domination. These false hypotheses of inferiority, assimilated by both exploited and exploiter, tend to seem natural. They strengthen the barriers of domination already artificially established. But when added together these barriers become more visible to the victims of discrimination.

Consciousness of this situation and of the mechanisms of perpetuation are increasing among some of the oppressed ethnic groups. At the same time they are finding a new identity through their specific struggles, and through their cultural backgrounds, which have built up over time a force of resistance and have nourished the hope for liberation which has been denied them because of economic realities. Therefore, the sense of racial identity and the sense of sexual identity have become strong forces for liberation.

The emancipation struggle to which Christians are committed should utilize for itself these forms and matrices which have seized the exploitation of classes. We theologians lack the necessary understanding in this field, although we form a part of it. Thus we should discuss and learn to understand the subtleties of race and sex discrimination, and

173

the importance of cultural differences among the oppressed races.

At the same time our understanding of the peculiarities of race and sex domination ought to contribute to our articulation with the details of our common struggle - worldwide - so we may help one another in organizing an effective force for today's dispossessed and oppressed. Thus the specific problems will be converted into a single common task. The building of a socialist society as an economic organization, with neither exploiters nor exploited, and having a culture of equality and solidarity, is our objective. This makes it imperative to note the danger of perpetuating intoned litanies of racism, sexism and culturalism while at the same time that we value and encourage the cultural attributes of ethnic groups.

As Christians we are committed to this struggle, lighting our activities with the Word of God which sustains an anthropological vision of all humanity being fundamentally equal in the sight of God. Such is the message from the opening of Genesis through the New Testament. The contribution of the Church would be neither sincere, nor Christian if within itself any form of race or sex discrimination were continued, however subtle. It is important for us in this sense to take very seriously the affirmation of Oaxtepec on the indigenous: "The churches of America ought to be stimulated to help native leaders learn Church administration of all levels, taking into consideration the cultural values of each ethnic group, as the basis for cultural, social and religious reality of the indigenous." (Oaxtepec, Op. cit., VI, VII).

For our part we committed ourselves to this integration during the meetings and in our reflection on the theology of liberation, where we ought to appreciate the presence and the contributions - on an increasing scale - of ethnic groups and of women, in order to find, all together, the roots of this global exploitation and to build the ways towards popular power.

Evangelization, Power and the State

The Christian accepts no form of domination of "person over person." In the political arena this domination is exercised simply because the people lack power. Political power based on an economic power which generates the appropriation of the fruit of another person's labor is one of the most terrible, most complicated and most difficult of realities to humanize. In the face of the complexity and importance of the problem, we can pretend to contribute only a basic reflection, which shows us the evangelical direction of the line indicated by Jesus for making power a service, not a lordship over others (Mark 10:42-45).

The state is the most effective instrument of power and through it the existing order seeks its own continuity. In capitalist societies, the dominant classes seek through the state to perpetuate the conditions for robbing the people. The state has exclusivity in exercising "legitimate violence;" the state makes and enforces the laws, in the name of the "common good." But those laws and regulations operate basically for the particular interests of the exploiting class. In order to hide this fact, the traditional or exploitative state elaborates an ideology which obscures its true objective and hides from view the reality of the class struggle - always imposed by the dominant class - by denying a truly human life to the oppressed. For this reason the traditional state develops political lines, such as social services, which mute the class struggle.

The economic power of the capitalist class - a reality which invades all social and political life - seeks and succeeds in converting religion so that it accepts its alliance through a legalistic ideological apparatus for domination, offering in exchange social privileges and support for its proselytizing task. Thus the religions, allied with the established power and with the state, convert themselves into those who consecrate and sanctify the established disorder.

In the face of this situation the struggle for liberation advances to the creation of the power of the people, which consists in increasing its capacity, its critical consciousness and its organization, until becoming able to determine the destinies of the whole collectivity, for the benefit of the people.

The alternative to this reality is the construction of a state identified with the masses and which is an institutional expression of the popular movement itself. This would mean a transformation of the economic organizations and of various aspects of social life, so that the workers become directors of their lives - a complete and permanent job, to which the

Christian ought to commit him/herself.

We Christians, in the name of the Evangelist, have the specific duty of delegitimizing all religion – particularly Christianity – which is identified with the oppressor state.

On the other hand, we ought to contribute to those activities of civil life and Church life which produce increased capacity, conscience and organization of popular alternatives, and we should support political expressions which seek those alternatives.

Furthermore we should work for the joining together and support by theological reflection and the social sciences of popular causes, in order in this way to collaborate in the construction of popular power.

Challenge and Perspective of Evangelization

Finally, we wish to express an overall concern about the tasks of evangelization in coming years vis-a-vis politics. How can the task of evangelization be made real, in relation to politics, in the various national situations to which we are committed? How can the task of evangelization make a real contribution to world politics?

First, Christianity is a constructor of peace and of justice; and the first great challenge to all humankind and to the Church, is their effective contribution to world peace. This is particularly important these dramatic days when the brutal attack on Viet Nam by China reminds us that the world rests on an arsenal of arms of enormous destructive power, maintained by ambitions of hegemony and by fear. The development and proliferation of nuclear arms is endangering all the life of the planet. The arms race is an act of not only war and politics, but also and essentially of economics. It indicates more and more that the economies of the developed nations are tiring from the race. The arms industries provide employment, and the exports contribute to the balance of payments. But also the arms race intensifies trade rivalries, provokes little wars among the underdeveloped nations and ruins their economies. These situations cannot be controlled by rhetoric, but obviously the imagination and initiative of Church members must be aroused so that they contribute to raise consciousness worldwide for taking concrete action against armaments.

Then as to the transnational enterprises, with their economic power spread over many nations – they tend to convert governments and people into simple instruments for serving them and assuring profit for their investors. Only a concerted political effort of governments and their people can control this menace.

The fundamental challenge is the profound impoverishment-economic, social, cultural and political- of the poor in the peripheral underdeveloped countries particularly. The opulence found in the developed countries of the center is related to this poverty. But when the poor become conscious of this and organize themselves, the established powers - national and international - react, putting into operation their programs of "national security" which, basically, means "security for the empire," in the name of which brutal repression by military forces is legitimized. The politics of national security is known also, of course, in the center of the empire.

With the failure of merely military solutions for guaranteeing the establishment of systems of domination, and once the military governments have disarticulated the popular organizations, have exiled many of their directors and imprisoned and assassinated others, they then launch campaigns for a "more humane face." The Trilateral Commission's politics are oriented in this line. Its fomenting of "controlled democracy" and of human rights is understood to mean only liberal political rights, leaving aside the gravest and most generalized violations of basic human rights of the oppressed.

The evangelical significance of politics requires us to identify ourselves with the masses, to the classes suffering from these types of manipulation, and to contribute to increasing their power.

In developed capitalist countries Christians should take up political tasks for attaining world peace and demobilizing the immense economic, political and social apparatus of armaments created by this terrible inhuman rationale. In countries now building socialism the Church has the ongoing duty of contributing to the socialist obligation of keeping the economics and politics of their land safely and constantly in the hands of the people, with no deviation.

In these tasks Christians express themselves as Children of God, in fraternal relationship with all humankind and their poverty of having nothing but the love of the Creator for the children of Creation. In this way their worship,

their prayers and their hopes for eschatological integrity
will not be alienated or justified by social disorder
but rather, they will be expressed by their truly Christian
lives in the building of the Kingdom of Heaven, in a new world
and under a new heaven, under a reign of justice, unity and
peace. Concrete accomplishments, historically within reach,
give us proof of a God ever more powerful, towards whom we
are traveling, as long as we continue to build community.

*   *   *

APPENDICES

FINAL REPORT OF THE MEETING

The International Meeting of Theologians, assembled under the theme of "Evangelization and Politics," was organized by the Latin American and Caribbean Christian Peace Conference in conjunction with the Evangelical Seminary of Theology in Mantanzas, Cuba, the site of the conference.

The participating theologians represented twenty-five countries:

1	Angola	1	Holland
1	Argentina	1	India
1	Belgium	6	Mexico
1	Bolivia	2	Mozambique
1	Brazil	1	Poland
2	Chile	4	Puerto Rico
2	Costa Rica	1	El Salvador
18	Cuba	2	Soviet Union
1	Czechoslovakia	6	The United States of
2	France		North America
1	German Democratic Republic	6	Venezuela
3	Federal Republic of Germany		
1	Hungary		

I. OPENING SESSION

President and chairperson: Rev. Gustavo Astudillo, vice president of the Latin American and Caribbean Christian Peace Conference. Also on the presidential platform were: Prof. Sergio Arce Martínez, Vice President of the Latin American and Christian Peace Conference and Rector of the Evangelical Seminary of Theology; Rev. Lubomir Mirejowsky, Secretary General of the International Christian Peace Conference; Rev. Raúl Fernández Ceballos, President of the Ecumenical Council of Cuba and Executive Secretary of the Latin American and Caribbean Christian Peace Conference; Dr. Raúl Gómez Treto, International Secretary of the Christian Peace Conference and adjunct Secretary of the Latin American and Caribbean Christian Peace Conference; Prof. Dora Valentín, Finance Secretary of the Latin American and Caribbean Christian Peace Conference; Rev. Augusto Cotto, President of the

181

Theological Committee of the Latin American and Caribbean
Christian Peace Conference; Father Carlos M. de Céspedes,
Secretary of the Cuban Bishops Conference and president of
the official Roman Catholic delegation to the Meeting.

The session opened with devotions led by Rev. Adolfo
Ham, Dean of Theology at the Evangelical Seminary of Theology,
followed by greetings from Dr. Sergio Arce Martínez, Father
Carlos Manuel de Céspedes, Rev. Raúl Fernández Ceballos, Rev.
Ludomir Mirejowsky, Mons. Manuel Viera Pinto and Rev. Augusto
Cotto. The message from Bishop Karóly Tóth, President of the
International Christian Peace Conference, was read.

II. PRESENTATIONS

Formal presentations of the problems of evangelization
under the political and economic situations of their respective countries were made by eleven of the delegates, nine of
which are included in this volume. Two others were presented
by Enrique Dussel of Argentina and Mons. Vieira of Mozambique.

Formal commentaries were offered by Prof. Harvey Cox,
Dr. Ignacio Castuera, Dr. Raúl Vidales, Rev. Ofelia Ortega,
Prof. W. Benedicktowicz, Prof. J. B. Metz and Prof. Hugo
Assmann. All of the formal discussion and the commentaries
were followed by full discussion from the floor. Simultan-
eous translation into several languages was provided for all
participants.

III. PANEL ON THE PUEBLA CONFERENCE

The Third Latin American Bishops Conference (CELAM III),
held in Puebla, Mexico, in early 1979 was summarized by Father
Marciano García, a member of the official Cuban delegation.
Other commentaries on CELAM III were offered by Enrique Dussel, Dr. Fernándo Danel and Father Alex Morelli. The far
reaching significance of the Bishops Conference was discussed
in detail.

IV. EXPOSITIONS ON VIET NAM AND VIEQUES

Father François Houtart presented an extraordinarily
vivid report on the present situation and recent history of
the Catholic Church in the Socialist Republic of Viet Nam.

Rev. Alberto González of Puerto Rico spoke on the present plight of the population of Vieques, an island off the southeast coast of Puerto Rico. He related the struggle there against militarism which is being waged by the directors and laity of the Pentecostal churches.

V. DISCUSSION GROUPS

Following the formal plenary presentations the participants divided into five groups for discussion and for drafting the Final Document of the meeting. The heterogeneity of these groups led effectively to concensus and facilitated informal and spontaneous expression. Through these frank discussions a better understanding of the variety of political and theological thinking in diverse areas around the world was gained.

VI. DEVOTIONS

Each day's work began with religious services in several languages, adapted to the topics scheduled for the day. The prayer, the selections of Bible readings and the hymns expressed the commitment and faith of the participants as they have been deepened in a variety of struggles for liberation.

VII. ENTERTAINMENT

The professional choir of Matanzas gave an evening concert of Cuban music on February 28.

On March 1 the folklore groups of singers and dancers, "Arará," of the city of Jovellanos presented and described various ritualistic and festive dances of the African slaves, brought to Cuba centuries ago, which today enrich the culture and popular music of the island.

The residence of Dora and Sergio Arce was open to the delegates and participants at all free times. Under informal and cordial atmosphere it was possible to discuss and ask questions about the proceedings. This opportunity for informal discussion was a great help in breaking down barriers of distance and also cultural differences.

VIII. DOCUMENTS

The Final Document was drafted by a committee elected by the plenary, based upon the summaries and conclusions of the five discussion groups. The draft was then discussed by the plenary. The most salient pronouncements of the meetings in Oaxtepec and Puebla were included.

The plenary approved statements on Mozambique, Viet Nam, the island of Vieques in Puerto Rico and on Nicaragua.

The plenary approved the sending of letters to Zamora Moisés Michel; Phan Vang Dong; the Catholic Patriotic Liaison Committee in Hanoi; Mons. Nguyen Van Binh in Ho Chi Minh City; the Christian Board of Churches of Viet Nam; and to Dr. Károly Tóth of the Christian Peace Conference in Prague, Czechoslovakia. A letter was also sent to the Secretary of the United Nations, Dr. Kurt Waldheim.

IX. CLOSING SESSION

The meeting ended March 2 with a devotional led by Rev. Nora Beatriz Quiroga of Bolivia. The service was a reflection on the dignity of women. The final assembly was addressed by Dr. Sergio Arce Martínez.

X. THE FINAL RECEPTION

The meeting formally ended with a reception for all those in attendance by the Instituto Cubano de Amistad con los Pueblos (ICAP), in the halls of the Library Antonio Guiteras in Matanzas. The guests were graciously received by Mario Rodríguez of the Advisory Board of the Presidency of ICAP, whose welcoming address centered on the necessity for close alliance between Christians and Marxists in the worldwide struggle for the liberation of humanity from exploitation and misery. He emphasized that this meeting - held in Cuba, the first socialist country in America - was a manifestation of that alliance.

Rev. Lubomir Mirejowsky, Secretary General of the Christian Peace Conference, responded by thanking him, the official institutions and the social and mass organizations of Cuba, for the hospitality and many attentions which the participants had received during the meetings.

Following the reception ICAP presented a display of

photographs demonstrating the accomplishments of the Cuban
revolution during the twenty years of construction of a new
society, with the cooperation of the Cuban people, whether
believers or non-believers. A final toast was offered.

*   *   *

REPORT OF THE CONTINUATION COMMITTEE

I

The Committee for Continuation of Work of the Latin American and Caribbean Christian Peace Conference met March 4-6 at the Evangelical Seminary of Matanzas, Cuba.

II

The presidency was occupied by Vice President Paulo Mar Gregorios, Metropolitan (India) and Rev. Sergio Arce Martinez (Cuba) of the CPC International. Rev. Lubomir Mirejowski (Czechoslovakia), the Secretary General of the CPC International, also helped preside.

III

Presiding over the Meeting were Bishop Jacinto Ordoñez (Costa Rica) and Presbyter Raul Fernandez Ceballos (Cuba), respectively president and secretary general of the Latin American and Caribbean Christian Peace Conference.

IV

We were honored by the presence of Bishop José Vieira Pinto, Roman Catholic Bishop of Nampula, Mozambique, who brought fraternal greetings to the meeting.

V

The plenary assembly noted with regret the absence of Brothers Mauricio Lopez and Heiber Conteris, who found it impossible to attend, and expressed the hope that they might be with us again.

VI

The central theme of the meeting "Evangelization and Politics" was presented by Rev. Ernle Gordon (Jamaica), Vice President of the Latin American and Caribbean Christian Peace Conference. Rev. Gordon analyzed thoroughly the relationship which exists between the rapid social and political changes taking place on our continents and the evangelical task of the Church. He affirmed that it is impossible to evangelize without knowing the people being evangelized and the political and economic realities of our respective nations. Evangelization, he said, should be global, and the CPC can be helpful in gaining these ends. Evangelization ought to be the result of a new interpretation of the entire program of Christian education in our churches.

The Church, he added, must be preoccupied with the construction
of a new society, and this society ought to be socialist.
Evangelization, concluded Rev. Gordon, should be revolutionary,
it should radicalize society. It should be based on the
quest for peace and for justice.

VII

The Secretary General of the Christian Peace Conference,
Rev. Dr. Lubomir Mirejovski, presented a detailed report on
the activities of the CPC in recent months, and of plans for
the current year. He stressed three points essential for
the work of the CPC in the near future:
  a) Development of the movement through support of the
     "base groups" (comunidades de base)
  b) Contacts with other groups and organizations, both
     Christian and non-Christian
  c) Inclusion of the CPC as one of the Non-Governmental
     Organizations of the United Nations (NGO's)

Many of Rev. Gordon's suggestions were discussed in detail.

VIII

A detailed report was presented on the work of the CPC in
Latin America in association with other ecumenical organizations, such as the CMI, CLAI, FUMEC, COPEC, CECOPE. The report noted activities for establishing solidarity with peoples
who are struggling for their liberation. Of special interest
was the Meeting of Women of the Americas (held in Matanzas)
and the recently concluded Meeting of Theologians (also held
in the Seminary in Matanzas).

IX

Other reports were presented on activities in different areas
of work, studies and promotion, and plans for future work
were outlined.

X

The invasion of the Democratic Republic of Viet Nam by the
Peiping Camarilla was condemned by a resolution and declara-
tions of support for the struggles of the people of Nicaragua,
Puerto Rico and El Salvador were expressed.
The Committee for Continuation of Work of the CPC sent letters
of salutation to Commander Fidel Castro, Mons. Sergio Mendez
Arceo, Lic. Raul Macin, Mons. Oscar Romero, Fr. Ernesto Card-
enal and to the Parliament of Sweden recommending Oscar Romero

as a candidate for the Nobel Peace Prize.
Declarations of support were sent for the Sixth Summit Meeting of the Non-Aligned Nations, which is to be held in Havana in September, 1979; for the International Day of the Child; and the International Conference being held in Helsinki on the Viet Nam struggle.

XI

The Committee expressed gratitude to all the individuals and organizations making possible the holding of the meeting.

*   *   *

PARTICIPANTS

Ajo, Joel - Cuba
Arce, Sergio - Cuba
Assmann, Hugo - Brazil
Astudillo, Gustavo - Venezuela
Bastián, Jean P. - México
Batista, Israel - Cuba
Benedicktowicz, Vitold - Poland
Boer, Dick - Holland
Brown, Robert McAfee - U.S.A.
Carvalho, Emilio de - Angola
Casalis, Dorotheé - France
Casalis, Georges - France
Camps, Carlos - Cuba
Castellanos, René - Cuba
Castillos, Fernando - Chile
Castillo, Ramón - Venezuela
Castuera, Ignacio - U.S.A.
Céspedes, Carlos - Cuba
Cone, James - U.S.A.
Cotto, Augusto - El Salvador
Cox, Harvey - U.S.A.
Danel, Fernando - México
David, René - Cuba
Dimas, Antonio - Portugal
Dusell, Enrique - Argentina
Fernández, Raúl - Cuba
Fink, Ilsegret - German Democratic Republic
Fomín, Sergei - U.S.S.R.
Garrido, José - Cuba
Gómez, Raúl - Cuba
González, Alberto - Puerto Rico
Gordon, Ernle - Jamaica
Ham, Adolfo - Cuba
Houtart, François - Belgium
Kroehler, Lois - Cuba
López de Silva, José - Mozambique
Machado, Juan M. - Cuba
Mar Gregorios, Paulos - India
Marichal, Odén - Cuba

189

Márquez, Fernando - Venezuela
Masuera, Migdaleder - Venezuela
Meńdez, Moisés - México
Metz, Johannes B. - Federal Republic of Germany
Mirejowski, Lubomir - Czechoslovakia
Morelli, Alex - México
Norniella, Francisco - Cuba
Novinski, Vasili - U.S.S.R.
Ordoñez, Jacinto - Costa Rica
Ortega, Ofelia - Cuba
Piedra, Carlos - Cuba
Pixley, Jorge - México
Quiroga-Boots, Nora - Bolivia/U.S.A.
Reyes, Gabriel - Chile
Rivera, Luis - Puerto Rico
Ruiz, María I. - Puerto Rico
Schmauch, Cristoph - U.S.A.
Stewart, Gordon - U.S.A.
Stock, Konrad - Federal Republic of Germany
Suárez, Angel - Venezuela
Szombathy, Ginla - Hungary
Tinidad, Saĺl - Costa Rica
Ugalde, Louis - Venezuela
Von Wartemberg, Barbel - Federal Republic of Germany
Valentín, Dora - Cuba
Vidales, Raúl - México
Vieira, Manuel - Mozambique
Villalón, José R. - Puerto Rico

Special Guests
González, José A. - Cuba
López, Enrique - Cuba
Rodríguez, Armando - Cuba

Observers
Brene, Arístides - Cuba
Ortiz, Remberto - Cuba
Paz, Juan Ramón de la - Cuba
Pérez, José F. - Cuba
Roccaro, Bruno - Cuba
Villalón, Luis - Cuba

Religious Press
García, Raimundo - Cuba

Cuban Staff
Ceballos, Elier
Cruz, Buenaventura
Gómez, Nacyra
González, Emmanuel
González, Orestes
Ham, Carlos
Herrera, Mercedes
Monteagudo, Modesta
Naranjo, Javier
Pérez, Miguel
Tabares, Tomás
Velar, Margarita

Sergio Arce Martinez – Cuba
>   Pastor, Reformed Presbyterian Church of Cuba
>   Rector and Professor of Systematic Theology
>   at the Evangelical Seminary of Theology in Matanzas.

Robert McAfee Brown – The United States of North America
>   Professor of Theology and Ethics
>   Pacific School of Religion, Berkeley.

Emilio de Carvalho – Angola
>   Bishop of the United Methodist Church of Angola.

George Casalis – France
>   Professor of Theology at the Protestant Theological
>   Faculty in Paris.

James H. Cone – The United States of North America
>   Professor of Systematic Theology at Union Theological
>   Seminary, New York.

Ilsegret Fink – German Democratic Republic
>   Pastor of the Evangelical United Church of the German
>   Democratic Republic.

Ernle Gordon – Jamaica
>   Rector of the Santa Maria Parish in Kingston, Jamaica.

François Houtart – Belgium
>   Professor of Sociology
>   Director of the Research Center for Social-Religious
>   Affairs at the Catholic University in Louvaine.
>   President of the Belgian-Viet Nam Association.

Paulos Mar Gregorios – India
>   Metropolitan of the Syrian Orthodox Church of India.
>   Rector and Professor of the Orthodox Seminary of Kerala.

*　　　　　*　　　　　*

THE CONFESSION OF FAITH

OF THE PRESBYTERIAN - REFORMED CHURCH

IN CUBA

PREFACE

0.01 The Presbyterian-Reformed Church in Cuba confesses its faith as it offers this testimony to the significance that the Gospel of Jesus Christ has today for the Church in Cuba.

0.02 The mere fact that this is done at this time and place is already an essential part of the proclamation of its faith in God, the Creator; of the reason for its hope in the Incarnate Son, the Reconcilor; and of the action of its love in the Holy Spirit, the Redeemer.

0.03 This testimony constitutes the affirmation of the joy which the Church of Jesus Christ experienpes in the Gospel as it lives this historic moment of humanity and especially as it proclaims the meaning that faith has for us in the midst of the Cuban revolutionary process.

0.04 God's Incarnation in Jesus of Nazareth and the liberating vocation this fact implies for the Church constitute the spiritual foundation for the historical commitment to which the Church feels it is called.

0.05 It is necessary for the Church to clarify the meaning of that commitment. As it does this, the Church gives the reason for its hope and lives its love confessing in this way its faith.

0.06 Obligated to carry out that commitment, the Church, by the Holy Spirit and through its own action, is nourished by the knowledge it needs to have about God's redeeming purpose in Jesus Christ as it is revealed in the Scriptures, norm of its faith, paradigm for its action.

0.07 The Presbyterian-Reformed Church in Cuba, with a profound sense of its apostolicity and catholicity, calls all

193

human beings to join in the task of realizing fully the new
humanity on the earth, which would mean the installation of a
fraternal and solidary community, which, including all alike,
achieves love as its supreme law. This fact constitutes the
only evangelical way of being able to know God, and thus of
proclaiming God to all human beings.

0.08 We, the members of this Church, join all believers
in Jesus Christ – praying for the coming of the Kingdom of God –
in the hope of its realization, and, strengthened in fraternal
love, we confess our faith as the Church of Jesus Christ in
Cuba.

SECTION I – THE CENTRALITY OF THE HUMAN BEING MADE KNOWN THROUGH JESUS CHRIST

1.01 The Church believes in God because it believes in
the human being, and believes in the human being because it
believes in Jesus Christ, the Son of God, our Older Brother.

1.02 This centrality of the human being in the faith of
the Church is presented within the framework of those two references which are very explicit and very clear; one, God, the
Creator of every human being; and the other, Jesus Christ, the
Old Brother Reconcilor of every human being. As we present
it in this way, we do not deny, but rather just the opposite,
we reaffirm both as essentials of the faith.

1.03 Faith in Jesus Christ obligates the Church to place
the human being in the center of its interest and concern, and
to consider Jesus as a parameter to judge all things, especially to evaluate its own doctrinal teaching, its specific
ecclesiastical structures and its particular mission as the
Church.

1.04 The Church considers that God in Jesus Christ reveals to us that the center of His interest, concern and value
judgment of all things, is in His human "creature," to the
point of "stripping himself bare" and becoming "flesh of sin"
for His redemption.

A – JESUS CHRIST: CENTER OF OUR INTEREST

1.A.01 The Church affirms that the center of its interest
is Jesus Christ.

194

1.A.02 The Church believes in Jesus Christ. In Jesus
Christ, in the human event of Jesus Christ, God reveals to us
His redeeming purpose.

1.A.03 In the historic realization of the Revelation in
Jesus Christ, God does not gaze in a tangential way on the concrete reality of the human being; but rather, on the contrary
God inserts itself in history, taking it on as God's own. In
that way God calls us all to fulfill ourselves as human beings
through concrete historic projects of Redemption.

1.A.04 The insertion of God in history requires of the
Diety that "he strip himself bare" and take on the form of
the oppressed one, "of a slave." This speaks, on the one
hand, of Love's sacrificial magnitude and on the other, of
its solidary magnitude.

1.A.05 When the Church proclaims that it believes in
Jesus Christ, it is affirming that to know God is to know
Jesus Christ, and that to know God in Jesus Christ is to know
truly the human being; because within the concrete and historic reality of the life of the Oppressed One, the Divine
is realized in its greatest possible human magnitude, showing
in turn the human meaning of the life which is lived unconditionally in, by and for other human beings.

1.A.06 When the Church teaches that Jesus Christ is the
Son of God, Our Older Brother, Incarnate and Resurrected,
"first born among many brothers and sisters," it is giving
the reason for its hope in the possibility of historically
realizing justice and peace in the world, since in His death
He overcomes the sin of injustices and hatreds and also overcomes the death of radical and incontrovertible frustrations.

1.A.07 When the Church lives its love for "Jesus Christ
and Him crucified," it takes on in full responsibility the
solution presented by God to the human problem through sacrificial and solidary love which works justice and establishes
peace.

B - THE HUMAN BEING: CENTER OF GOD'S INTEREST
1.B.01 The Scriptures give witness to the fact that the

human being is the center of all God's interest. All through
the pages of the Bible, God's love for the creature is not
only made evident, but it is also presented as a divine necessity. God's loving interest in the human creature is identified in the Scriptures as God's very essence.

1.B.02 The Church finds in this Love, and only in it,
all the theological material with which to formulate doctrinal truths. The doctrinal development of the Church and
all the doctrines it has elaborated in its theologial under-
takings through the centunies, are valid to the extent that
they express better God's loving purpose for the human being.

1.B.03 When the Church emphasizes the doctrines of Incarnation and Atonement, it witnesses to God's love for the
human being, since it proclaims the magnitude of His sacrificial and solidary nature.

1.B.04 In this way, the Church raises God's interest and
concern and evaluation of all things centered in the human
being, to the level of a divine necessity, interpreting correctly what the Scriptures teach us about His "Nature" and
"Attributes."

C - THE HUMAN BEING: CENTER OF THE CHURCH'S INTEREST IN
    JESUS CHRIST
1.C.01 The Church, on being interested in Jesus Christ
and only in Jesus Christ and Him crucified and risen from the
dead, centers its interest in the human being.

1.C.02 The Church's faithfulness to Jesus Christ ties
it to the historic commitment of its Lord, a commitment of
human Redemption through sacrificial, solidary and unconditional Love for the human being.

1.C.03 When the Church proclaims that Jesus Christ is
the "Incarnate Son of God," and our "Risen Old Brother," it
witnesses to the fact that sacrificial and solidary Love is
not only a divine necessity, but also a human necessity, "sign"
of the "mystery of God" and of the "mystery of the human being."

1.C.04 When the Church teaches that the Scriptures witness to the supreme value God places on the human creature,
becoming his/her Creator, Reconcilor and Redeemer, it recognizes the fact that sacrificial and solidary and unconditional
Love for the human being constitutes its own and only necessity.

1.C.05 The Church recognizes that sacrificial, solidary
and unconditional Love is necessary for it to be the Church
of Jesus Christ; and, espousing the cause of human dignity
and decorum in every moment and in whatever place as its only
reason for being, without placing any condition on its commitment, and without having it matter what the circumstances
are in which it lives or the risks which it runs, it participates fully in human Redemption.

1.C.06 When the Church lives like this, it is living in
God, by God and for God. To serve and love God in Jesus
Christ is for the Church to center its interest, its concern
and evaluation of all things in the human being, accepting
that the Christological form of being is the only way for
God to become accessible to the Creature and the only way for
the Church to make itself acceptable to God and to other human beings.

1.C.07 If the Church should stop existing for, by and
in the human being, it would stop being the Church of Jesus
Christ, the Son of God and our Older Brother.

1.C.08 When the Church lives its historical reality
placing the human being in the very center of its interest in
Jesus Christ, it does not lose its identity as the "body of
Christ" or as "Christ's bride," but all the contrary; even
in its greatest degree of secularization the Church achieves
the realization of its irrenunciable commitment of serving
and loving Jesus Christ, since in Him, at His own expense,
God is secularized radically and unconditionally in His redemptive task of working for the fullness of the decorum and
dignity of all human beings.

SECTION II - THE HUMAN BEING: AN "ECONOME"
2.01 The Scriptures teach us that the human being is
characterized by being an "econome" of all things, God's

197

steward. All goods, both material and spiritual, that we obtain as persons or as nations, cannot be considered in the
final analysis as "individual" nor "national" property in
an exclusive way, be it individualist, classicist, elitist
or nationalist. Even less can they have a transcendent
value which, by reason of the "natural law" or the "divine
law," has been given goods as "private ownership of the
means of production."

2.02 To make human spiritual essence depend on the exercising of the so-called "right to private property," constitutes one of the most tragic aberration - because of its consequences - the human spirituality has suffered to this day.

2.03 The Scriptures teach us that the human being will
be that which s/he is able to do and become as an "econome."
The "econome" (oikonomos) is the one most used in the New
Testament when it is a matter of judging the achievements of
human life. In the Old Testament the term "econome" (mensha-
la) is given equal importance.

2.04 When the Marxists insist on the "economical" as the
basic element, fundamental for interpreting the significance
of human life as it is developed in its history, they make the
Church - one of those ironies of history - reconsider the Biblical criterion of the human being as an "econome."

2.05 The Church proclaims that the human vocation is
that of being a "good econome." The "house" that the human
creature administers is the whole world of Creation; and each
person is responsible for it to other creatures who are co-
inhabitants and to God.

2.06 The responsibility of creating goods and adminis-
trating them is the first right of every human being, the
essential principle of his/her spirituality. The Church
teaches that each and every human being should share responsibly in the mutual exercise of that right. To violate that
right is the first criminal act against human dignity and decorum.

2.07 The most perfect social system will be the one that

guarantees the responsible participation of all citizens in the matters of "public administration." The effect respect for that right is necessary in order for the society to be made up of persons and not sub-human individuals. Such is the real principle of true "demo-cracy".

2.08 The Church teaches that the committed participation of its members in public life, in the administration of its economy, is not something one can choose to add or not to add to his/her condition of believer; on the contrary, the responsible exercise of this right is an integral and inseparable part of the loving practice of the Christian faith.

2.09 Therefore the Church teaches that it is an integral part of the life of the Christian believer to exercise his/her rights and to fulfill his/her duties as a citizen, especially in our case, where the democracy is made effective through the constitution of the Popular Power and the worker-syndical participation in the places of work.

2.10 The aberrations of a "faith" which calls itself a-apolitical are of such consequence for the falsification o human spirituality and the meaning of the social nature of life that the Church, indignant, rejects them and combats them as "heretical." Only an interested distortion of the faith - against all argumentation grounded on scriptural truth-can make the simple Christian believer renounce the struggle and effort to find, together with his fellow countrymen, the most adequate solutions to the problems patent in the neighborhood, in the city or in the nation, and keep him/her from enriching the life of all and making it more decorously human through a better "economy" of his/her time, abilities, knowledge and the goods produced.

A - WORK: PRINCIPLE OF HUMAN SPIRITUALITY
2.A.01 The Scriptures teach us that work is the means through which we exercise our vocation as "econimes," both in the creation of material and spiritual goods but also in their "good" administration.

2.A.02 The Scriptures teach us also that when we affirm that the human being is primarily a worker, we are proclaiming

that s/he is created "in the image and likeness of God" to
"work for six days" so that s/he can "rest the seventh." In
the New Testament we are called to be workers "in the image
and likeness of Christ." God and Christ, "one and the same
thing," the content of which is defined by Jesus himself:
"My Father works and I work." In the New Testament they go
so far as to deny the right to eat – which is like denying
the right to live – to anyone "who will not work."

2.A.03 In the Old Testament we are also ordered to exercise dominion and control over all things so that we be
the "image and likeness of God." In the New Testament we are
called to be no longer "slaves" that carry out the "order" to
work, but rather "friends" of Jesus Christ working freely
God's will.

2.A.04 The Church is faithful to the Scriptures and to
the Gospel when it invites all human beings, and especially
Christian believers, to enter into the historical project of
"dominating" nature through creative work and the administration of goods produced. These human activities are to be
exercised in such a way that justice and peace are established
in the world as the only manifestation of God's redeeming,
sacrificial and solidary love for all human beings.

B – BEING IN COMMUNITY: SPECIFICITY OF THAT WHICH IS HUMAN

2.B.01 The human being is a social being. The Scriptures teach that the social nature of the human being is an
essential part of his/her existence "in the image and likeness
of God."

2.B.02 The human being is a "political being." The
Scriptures teach that to be human is to live in community and
in a community structured in some form. The fact of the life
and death of Jesus Christ exemplifies for the Church how decisive the specific social-political nature of the human being
is for God.

2.B.03 The "secret" of the full social-political life –
which makes possible the fulfillment of the vocation of the
human being-econome – is revealed in Jesus Christ, who "came

200

not to be served, but to serve and give His life as a ransom
for His people."

2.B.04 Therefore the Church proclaims that wherever
there is a genuine and effective service of human recuperation, living sacrificial and solidary Love, unconditioned and
unrestricted for others, there Jesus Christ is present. His
presence has only one identification, "I am among you as one
who serves."

2.B.05 The Church teaches that creative work and the
administrative task accompanying it, must be presided over by
the fraternal community spirit, making all human beings brothers and sisters in the political activity that makes all
"better economes" every day.

2.B.06 The Church, in its members, lives the community
action (KOINONIA) of the Holy Spirit that makes us "companions"
(KOINONOS) of our neighbors and God's "coadjutors" in the task
of human redemption, when said members are realized as "faithful" economes before God and before their neighbors.

C - FREEDOM: HUMAN RESPONSIBILITY

2.C.01 The Scriptures teach that the human being, different from any other creature, is a "free being." Human
freedom, however, is a "responsible freedom." According to
the Scriptures, human freedom is not doing what one wishes
"out of whim or conceit." Neither is it the "free will" of
the philosophers. The Bible teaches that human freedom is
responsible, voluntary and conscious obedience to the Divine
Will.

2.C.02 The Will of God - as it is described in the Bible -
is a Will of loving Grace for the creature. God's loving
Grace for the human being is revealed concretely in the realization of Justice and Peace in the world, in the establishment of the Kingdom of Freedom and Love, the Kingdom of God.

2.C.03 Therefore, the Church proclaims that the human
being is "predestined to be free."

2.C.04 The Church teaches that we will be free to the

201

extent which we obey the loving Will of God serving effectively the cause of Justice and Peace among all human beings.

2.C.05 The Church lives in a real and concrete practice of human freedom on the part of the members as they become committed participants in the quantitative growth and the qualitative development of "love-justice" in the social, political and economic structures of human society, including the very structures of the Church as a social-juridical institution.

D - THE HUMAN BEING ECONOME: CENTER OF THE INTEREST OF THE CHURCH

2.D.01 The human being according to the Scriptures, is the "econome" which serves God in service to his/her neighbors in all tasks of human redemption. All the parables Jesus uses to judge our human situation and condition take as an evaluative norm the fidelity of the human being to his/her vocation of "econome."

2.D.02 The Church therefore does not support nor serve the interests of the oppressing classes that rob the human being of his/her vocation to be responsibly free economes by exploiting the work of the many to increase the riches of the few at the expense of the generalized increase of human misery, a "sign" of the frustration of God's love.

2.D.03 The Church proclaims that human beings, as persons and as nations, "are to work with their own hands to have something to give to those in need," fulfilling thus their vocation as "economes."

2.D.04 The Church teaches the seriousness of what is involved in the human historical process, both in that which has to do with personal particularity and with general universality. For the Church, what is involved is precisely the full realization of God's redeeming purpose in Nature, History and Human Conscience; that is, the Coming of the Kingdom of God.

2.D.05 The Church lives its Love centered in the human being, in the measure in which its members really become a "community of economes" who feel responsible before God to try

to live their condition of human beings genuinely in complete
fulfillment of their responsibilities in the Redemption of
Nature, History and Human Conscience.

SECTION III - HISTORY: INTEGRATING RECONSTRUCTION OF THE HUMAN BEING

3.01 The Scriptures teach us that the human being has
been converted into an explicit contender against the Redeeming purpose of God. "Sin" blurs the "image and likeness of
God" in the creature. The Bible also tells us that in Jesus
Christ, God reconciles the human being with this Redeeming
purpose.

3.02 All human history is illuminated in this way as a
process of integrating reconstruction of the human being.
This process, for the Scriptures, does not march forward in
a straight lineal form, but presents its great ups and downs.
Biblical History continually shows us the ascendent and
descendent direction that this process takes on.

3.03 In the Scriptures, what is called "sin" is the historical and concrete forms adopted by those "inferior moments"
within the process of human redemption. "Sin" imposes "pain"
and "sweat" on the human being in the process of his/her History, under the sign of "death."

3.04 The Church proclaims the fidelity of God to the
creature, fidelity which is manifested in the continuous call
of God to all human beings to overcome thier "disintegration"
of sin and death. God, "with strands of love," binds all
those who hear this call and follow God, to the Divine Creating, Reconciling and Redeeming work.

3.05 The Church teaches that in the Life, Death and Resurrection and Ascension of Jesus Christ, God puts an end to
the disintegrating power of sin and death, and opens the possibility of salvation for all humankind.

3.06 The Church lives in the militant and committed
participation of each one of its members in the task of the
integrating Reconstruction of the human being. This Reconstruction touches each person in its spiritual, social, economical and ecological totality.

A - THE HUMAN BEING: A BEING DISINTEGRATED BY SIN

3.A.01 The Bible teaches us that in "sin" there is a disintegrating disfigurement that acts on human life, tragically frustrating it both in its universal and its personal aspects.

3.A.02 "Sin" is the aberrant disintegrating distortion that transforms human work - the very principle of human spirituality - into an accursed task imposed on us for subsistence in societies characterized by competition and discrimination.

3.A.03 "Sin" is the aberrant disintegrating distortion that transforms social-political life - the very specificity of the human being in community - into a battleground where hatred and jealousy, envy and selfishness produce fratricidal struggle, crime and the "exploitation of person by person."

3.A.04 "Sin" is the aberrant disintegrating distortion that transforms freedom - the responsibility of obeying the absolute demands of Love-Justice - into the slavery which affirms exclusively the particularized interest of our "individuality," "race" or "nationality" in detriment of the dignity and decorum of others, and therefore, to our own detriment as persons, races or nations.

3.A.05 "Sin" is the aberrant disintegrating distortion that transforms material and spiritual goods, gifts of God and human achievements - for the usefulness of all alike - into factors of contradictions and discriminations among human beings through class-divided social structures. These factors reach the very altar of the Church, the altar of the Creator of all human beings.

3.A.06 Therefore the Church knows that because of "sin," work has been converted into a frustrated and frustrating activity which "separates" us fundamentally from our own vocation as "economes" and therefore makes us enemies of God, the Creator. Because of "sin," life in community has been converted into a dehumanized and dehumanizing jungle which "separates" us fundamentally from our neighbors, our brothers and sisters, and therefore makes us enemies of Jesus Christ, Reconcilor. And because of "sin," freedom has been converted

204

into an anarchy which, trying to pillage Nature and exploit our Neighbor, "separates" us fundamentally from the work of our hands, and therefore makes us enemies of the Holy Spirit, the Redeeming Presence of God, the Creator, and Jesus Christ, the Reconcilor.

3.A.07 The Church proclaims the human possibility of reconstruction beyond "sin" because of the faithfulness of God, who, in sacrificial and solidary Love, unconditional and unrestricted, offers us "forgiveness" in Jesus Christ.

3.A.08 The Church teaches that the Written Word reveals to us that the political, social and economic liberation of the Hebrew people, exploited and oppressed under the domination of Egypt, resulted in being the explicit, concrete and valid expression of their salvation, which constituted them as "God's People." In that very same way the "living and active" Word reveals to us that the victorious struggle for the political, social and economic liberation from the exploitation with which capitalist, monopolist and imperialist interest oppress the underdeveloped peoples of today, is the explicit, concrete and valid expression of their salvation which constitute them as God's New Humanity. This teaching of the Church does not contradict, but on the contrary, reaffirms and gives meaning to the Gospel proclaimed by Jesus Christ as it is revealed in the Scriptures.

3.A.09 The Church lives in its members when they contribute in a real way and with concrete historic actions to the disappearance of the "old Adam," disintegrated by "sin" and "death." The Church realizes thus – and not in any other way– its true Catholicity and Apostolicty as the "Body of Christ," "the Bride of the Lamb," the "People of God," according to the evangelical teaching.

B – SALVATION: <u>THE HISTORY OF THE SPIRITUAL</u>
<u>RECONSTRUCTION OF THE HUMAN BEING</u>

3.B.01 Salvation as the history of the spiritual reconstruction of the human being is a required theme of Christian preaching, a specific expression of Christian faith, hope and love.

3.B.02 Jesus Christ describes this spiritual reconstruction as the "birth of a new person." The assured possibility-
that the "old Adam" disintegrated by "sin," will "die" to give
way to a "new person," who will have eternal life - is affirmed
in the New Testament in terms of a "new creation," a "new
creature" when it is said that "the old things have all passed
away and everything is made new."

3.B.03 The "new person" does not stop being "human,"
but just the opposite. S/he is a human being who, having been
"born again," can then realize full humanity, liberated from
the chains that bound him/her irremissibly to the anti-human,
sinful past. The condition of "econome" does not change; it
is just that before the new person there opens up a "narrow
way" which leads to his/her being fully "an open door that no
one can close."

3.B.04 Creative work which makes it possible for the
human being to be like God, the principle of genuine spirituality, transfroms the person in a true and faithful "lieu-
tenant of God;" like the Older Brother. The pedagogical nature of work, a theme so highly esteemed by our Reformed
Founders, is affirmed when work is given, in the reconstruction of the human being, its fundamental spiritual value.

3.B.05 The Church proclaims the urgency for all human
beings, and especially Christian believers, to "discern the
time," in which they live, a "time to rise up from sleep"
and wake up to the reality that "we are now closer to the day
of our salvation than when we believed."

3.B.06 The Church teaches that the present "time" is
the time of judgment of "death" over the sins of an unjust
and cruel structural order that has exploited, for the benefit of only a few, the "vices" of the "old Adam" on which it
has sustained itself. The working class, precisely because
it is the working class, has been constituted in this "time,"
"time to rise up from sleep," in the legitimate standard
bearers of the construction of the new order which is more
human and just for all. If Jesus of Nazareth, the Son of
God and Our Older Brother, was a manual worker, and if the
ethics of the "new person" in the teaching of the New Testament

states that work is an essential element of the "holiness and righteousness according to God," then the Church can proclaim with all certainty and assurance, if it wants to be faithful to the Gospel, that "we are nearer today to the day of our salvation than when we believed."

3.B.07 The Church teaches – to be faithful to the Gospel – that Jesus Christ took the side of the oppressed and exploited class of his time and that "social-political" option took him, objectively speaking, to the Cross.

3.B.08 The Church lives in its members when they, faithful to the Gospel and to their Lord and knowing that it is not possible to serve two masters, repudiate service to God-Money. The Church is thus freed from the oppressive power with which the ideologies of domination and exploitation to this day have kept it captive, especially when under the imperialist political-cultural power, the Church is aware of how the greatest enemies of the human being today, and therefore, the greatest enemies of God, try to use it to defend their anti-Christian interests.

C – SALVATION: THE HISTORY OF THE SOCIAL-ECONOMIC RECONSTRUCTION OF THE HUMAN BEING

3.C.01 Salvation for the Scriptures means the reconstruction of the human being as "co-heir of all things;" that is, of those goods which, in faithfulness to his/her vocation as "econome," s/he has, with his/her work, co-created or re-created. Salvation is also, thus, the History of the Reconstruction of his/her being in community.

3.C.02 The "creation" of a "new person" means the establishment of a new community life in the new society, where there is no place for the exploitation of the work of another nor for racial discrimination nor the subjection of women as objects of mercantile, commerical or sexual consumption; nor will there be tolerance for the self-interested use of the legitimate values of family life in benefit of the false interests of the classist and discriminatory society.

3.C.03 The Scriptures teach us that salvation necessarily includes the emerging of a new fraternal solidarity that is made concrete in a "community of goods" where "private property" is abolished in order for all of us to be able to enjoy the goods produced.

3.C.04 The Bible teaches us, in the Old Testament, that a liberating process involves "as is written, that s/he who gathers much has nothing left over nor s/he who gathers little has lack." In the New Testament we are shown in a reliable way that the liberating fact of the Gospel, accepted fully, has an inevitable consequence that, "uniting us all" ideologically, we "have all things in common," receiving "each one according to his/her need."

3.C.05 The Church proclaims, following the Biblical-prophetic line carried to its final expression in Jesus Christ, that the entrance to the Kingdom is closed to the "rich," to the extent that their riches are the products of violence and injustice; and, in a specific way, it points out to all, and especially to the Christian believers, the fact that the capitalist system of social organization, in order to endure, has to maintian a manipulated and enslaving education that produces egoists who distort the meaning of human life and see as the supreme ideals of human life, unending consumption, the insatiable satisfaction of getting rich, the materialist fetichism and the drive for luxury and ostentation. As a result, this brings about a dehumanized society where the most ferocious competition is of utmost importance and in which its victims are inculcated social evasion by means of drugs, sexual excesses, gambling and alienating religiosity.

3.C.06 The Church teaches, according to its best reformed tradition, that "God desires that there be such identification and equality among us that each one help...according to his/her capacities, so that some do not have things left over while others are in need...that possessions and other goods be distributed according to the needs of each one."

3.C.07 The Church teaches that in the stability of the Government – in spite of its necessry ambiguities – we can find a guarantee for the administration of Justice and the maintenance of Peace when it is a case of "non-classist" societies,

where the power of the state is not in the hands of exploiting and oppressing classes, but in the hands of the workers.

3.C.08 The Church lives in the same measure in which
each one of its members works for the social-economical reconstruction of the human being within the Socialist State;
because, of all the historical forms of State known and ex-
perimented to this day, it is the society organized with such
(socialist) structures which offers the most concrete possibilities for making workable a more and more fairly distributive justice, which progressively reaches all citizens with
greater efficiency.

D - SALVATION: THE HISTORY OF THE ECOLOGICAL RECONSTRUCTION OF THE HUMAN BEING

3.D.01 "Sin," according to the Bible, distorts the human
being's relationships with Nature. The human being converted
into an unscrupulous pillager of natural resources, not only
has abused them, but also has made a diabolic use of them,
making them a part of exploitation, oppression and domination
of his/her fellow creatures.

3.D.02 The human being has pathologically altered the
development of Nature and has become, not its guardian, but
its perverter. Doing this, s/he has upset and damaged his/
her own human nature from a biological point of view. As a
psychic-social-somatic unit, given the complexity of human
nature, the human being has found him/herself affected in
biological development as well as in psychic health and social
promotion.

3.D.03 Nevertheless, the Church affirms that the technical-scientific activities of the human being, in his/her
eagerness to dominate and control Nature, do not work against
God's redeeming purpose which proposes - according to the Scriptures - "to put all things under God's feet." The "way" of
salvation that God opens in Jesus Christ, includes the full
realization of that domination and control. The Bible uses
the same word "health" for "salvation" and "liberation." We
cannot overlook the fact that in order to achieve a better
human "health" both in the biological and in the psychic and
social sense, it is necessary to control Nature more perfectly
and dominate its "mysteries" more completely.

3.D.04 The Church proclaims that, although it is an extremely secularized and secularizing society we are dealing
with, this does not mean that God would be absent from it;
rather it would mean the opposite. To believe in the doctrine
of the Incarnation means we believe in a God radically secularized in Jesus of Nazareth as the only way to the possibility of human Redemption.

3.D.05 The Church teaches that the human technological
undertaking serves to help create a new humanity to the extent
it makes achievable a greater deepening of human spirituality
with the disappearance of work as "exploitation."

3.D.06 The Church teaches that modern technology, when
it is at the service of the interests of exploiting classes,
has produced a series of false idols, such as utilitarian
logic, the reification of human beings and technocratic nihil-
ism. All Christian believers should fight committedly - together with those who strive to eradicate such idols - for
the disappearance of their "creators."

3.D.07 The Church teaches that, when our people chose
the Marxist-Leninist way of development through a social-political revolution, a more human relationship with Nature has
been brought about as well as a primary concern for the Health
of the people. The Marxist-Leninist Revolutuion has proved
to be the only way which makes the technological and ecological development possible and which successfully puts an end
to underdevelopment. This phenomenon of underdevelopment has
produced sub-human beings, victims of exploitation and oppression within the world capitalist and imperialist system.

3.D.08 The Church joyfully lives in the midst of the
Socialist Revolution, since the Revolution has concretely and
historically inaugurated a series of values in human relations
that make possible the whole modern technical-scientific development at the service of the full dignity of the human
being.

E- THE INTEGRAL HUMAN BEING: CENTER OF THE CHURCH'S
INTEREST IN HISTORY
3.E.01 The Church is interested specifically in human

210

history not only because for almost 2,000 years it has been
an important part of its development, but, principally because
it is precisely within the process of human history where God
in Jesus Christ has proposed to reconstruct the human being
integrally. To cut up that reconstruction into sections has
been the temptation the Church has fallen into as a consequence of the ideological captivity in which it has been en-
gulfed for centuries, putting itself at the service of the
exploiting classes, especially in the period of Monopoly
Capitalism.

3.E.02 The Church proclaims that there is only one History, and therefore it is not so much concerned about guaranteeing its own interests in the institutional-ecclesiastical
order, inherited from the past, as about assuring the readiness and willingness of its members to respond freely "with
the glorious freedom of the children of God" to the historical
demands that God makes on them in the conquest of a society
in which the integrally reconstructed human being - which is
the purpose of the Gospel - can emerge little by little.

3.E.03 The Church teaches that the "atheism" of the
ideology sustained by the Socialist Revolution, makes more
clearly evident the atheism of the "believers" who are not
capable of "discerning the signs of the times" in the midst
of the new society being constructed, in which the radical
transformations of the unjust structures make possible the
creation of a more integrally reconstructed human being.
The most important thing, in this case, is that the atheist-
communists serve as an inspiration to us because of their
readiness and willingness to live sacrificial, solidary
and effective Love.

3.E.04 The Church should be juridically separated from
the State. This does not mean however that the Church relin-
quishes its historical-political responsibility nor that the
Christian believers should withhold their most decided contribution to the construction of the new Socialist Society.

3.E.05 The Church lives this new situation without fears,
proclaiming the truth of the Gospel, confiding only in its
Lord and captive only of Jesus Christ. In that way it finds

its place in the human-historical process of integral recuperation. To do this the Church does not begrudge any sacrifices that may be necessary to fulfill its mission, whose
special characteristics vary in accordance with the moment
and the place it has to live.

3.E.06 The Church lives through the concrete love practiced by its members when they serve the socialist society
without hostility, trusting the divine-human sense of History and trusting the future which envisions a more effective
peace among nations and a more real justice among human
beings.

SECTION IV - THE KINGDOM OF GOD AND THE FULLNESS OF
               HISTORY

4.01 The Scriptures teach that the Kingdom of God is
inaugurated in History in Jesus Christ in an inescapable and
indefectible way. His birth as one of the poor of the Kingdom,
his class option as a worker for the Kingdom, his evangelizing Preaching as a prophet of the Kingdom, his life as a
neighbor of the Kingdom, his death as a Reconcilor for the
Kingdom, constitute him in the Kingdom itself. Today the
Kingdom is present among human beings through the action of
His Spirit, His Holy Spirit.

4.02 These realities of faith constitute the foundation
of the hope of the Church and the reason for its commitment
of unlimited and unconditional Love, to which it is bound in
the search for justice and peace in the world.

4.03 The Church - which has elaborated doctrines such as
the doctrine of Incarnation, of Atonement, of Resurrection -
rejects all dualism that leads to understanding human history
divided into two sections, one profane and another religious.

4.04 The Church proclaims its faith in the final coming
of the Kingdom grounded on the "mystery of the will" of God,
who "according to God's purpose set forth in Jesus Christ, at
the fullness of time, to unite all things in Christ."

A - THE DYNAMIC FORCE OF HISTORY
4.A.01 The Scriptures teach, typifying in the history

of "God's People," the way in which human history is constituted as "history of salvation" through a series of experiences in which the people grow in their awareness of the universal and totalizing nature of human Redemption.

4.A.02 The Biblical stories of Salvation – from Noah to
Jesus Christ, passing through Abraham and Sarah, Moses, David
and all the prophets and leaders of the Hebrew people before
and after the Babylonian Exile – show that the Church can teach
without fear of going wrong that the characteristic conflic-
tivity of the political, economic and social process of liberation energizes human history.

4.A.03 The class struggle that is manifested in the Bible
in the contradiction evidenced between oppressors and oppressed, between "just" and "unjust," between the rich that exploit and the exploited poor, together with the proclamation
of God as "Realizer of Justice" obligate the Church to accept
the close relationship between the Kingdom of God for which
we pray and the realization of Justice, and therefore of
peace, in the world.

4.A.04 The Church proclaims that God "Realizer of Justice" "abides in us in Love", in the effective love that con-
tributes to making the redeeming purpose of God for the human
being a reality shared by all, starting in this "now" and
this "here."

B – THE KINGDOM THAT ADVANCES
4.B.01 The Scriptures illustrate the Kingdom of God in
various ways. Sometimes, it is like a small seed that, once
sown, grows to be a leafy tree. On other occasions, it is
like a field of wheat in which the enemy sows tares. These
evangelical images teach us that behind the incessant and
constant process of struggles and contradictions which ener-
gize history, a development of irrecusable permanent value is
realized.

4.B.02 The Church proclaims that the Kingdom of God
grows constantly and that the achievements of justice and
peace in the world are achievements that fit into the Kingdom
as Fullness of History. The Church is the place where the

213

hope of a full realization of human life is cultivated in all
its creativity and solidarity, as an expression of the "glorious freedom of the children of God" who are "loaded with
fruits of justice."

4.B.03 The Church joyfully teaches that the New Socialist
Constitution of our country beholds the establishment of a more
just society when it affirms that "the first law of our Republic is the homage of the Cubans to the full dignity of the
person."

4.B.04 The Church teaches that the new meaning which
family relations have acquired - as it is expressed in the New
Family Code - reflects a step forward in the reconstruction of
the family life so necessary in the world of today.

4.B.05 The Church lives in the responsible participation of its members in the construction of the New Society
through all its activities: in the Committees of Defense of
the Revolution, in the Labor Unions, in the Federation of
Cuban Women, in the Organizations of Pioneers, of Students,
of Peasants; in every effort and work carried out to create
a new society of producers and not just consumers, where there
is a place therefore for the creation of a new kind of human
being, for whom love is no longer a Sunday commandment, but
rather the law which governs all his/her daily actions.

4.B.06 The Church proclaims that Peace is Possible in
the world. The Scriptures teach us that Peace (Shalom) is
not, in its essence, the absence of war, but the presence of
justice. The Church prays for Peace and works for Peace,
and doing so fulfills its mission as the Church of Jesus
Christ, the "Prince of Peace".

4.B.07 The Church joyfully teaches that the consolidation and development of the "socialist camp" in the world today and the policy of peace that its peoples and governments
set forth as an essential part of socialism, as well as the
extension and depth which the liberating anti-imperialist
struggles have acquired in the exploited peoples of the so-
called "Third World" all constitute "signs of the times" which
point toward a real possibility of achieving a world of greater
justice in relations between nations.

4.B.08   The Church lives in the responsible and committed work of its members who join in the struggles to halt the present arms race, to achieve the total disappearance of all testing of weapons of mass destruction and the establishment of complete disarmament in the world. In a world where there exist a United Nations Organization and a Helsinki Accord of Pacific and Cooperative Relations Among Nations, it becomes necessary for all governmnet and non-government organizations to make a special effort to guarantee all peoples the achievement of their full and responsible participation in the creation of a world which is more just and more nobly human. The Church is called to take part in this effort because of its very nature and mission.

4.B.09   The Church lives concretely in the intimate relations which exist between the coming of Jesus Christ the Savior and the definitive achievement of "Peace on Earth Among People of Good Will," the announcement of His coming.

4.B.10   Thus the Church is committed to the ecumenical struggle for the unity and peace of the whole Catholic Church, with the understanding that such efforts, in order to be genuine, must be realized as "signs" of our commitment to the struggle for the unity and peace of all humanity. In this sense we live our ecumenical task within the different organizations and movements to which we belong up until now (Cuban Ecumenical Council, World Alliance of Reformed Churches, Christian Peace Conference, World Council of Churches) and we support every effort for the achievement of such unity and peace in the "body of Christ."

C - THE KINGDOM: CENTER OF THE CHURCH'S INTEREST IN GOD
4.C.01   The Scriptures urge us to pray for the Kingdom, to preach its imminence, to teach its hope, to live its norms. The Church speaks of God by proclaiming the Reality of God, teaching God's truth and living God's Will.

4.C.02   The ultimate interest of the Church in God is not the interest in maintaining a particular type of worship, in propagating a precise "idea," in defending a specific "religion." The ultimate interest of the Church in God is the interest in the Kingdom of God.

4.C.03 The Church that is identified as the Church of Jesus Christ is constituted as the advance guard of the King-dom, because in Him, by Him and for Him "the Kingdom is among us" and it is not just a case of "it will come."

4.C.04 The Scriptures teach us that the "Kingdom is Peace, Justice and Joy in the Holy Spirit," the "convincer of all sin, of all justice and of all judgment." The Scrip-tures teach us that "to speak by the Spirit" is "to Prophesy."

4.C.05 The Church "prophesies" when it denounces that inside and outside of the new society we are building, there exist ideological currents that want to destroy it. They are strongholds, in the first case, of the interiorization of the vices of a past in which selfishness, hatred and competition were cultivated as "values" of the human spirit; enemies, in the second case, which, setting up such human anti-values, present themselves falsely as standard bearers of Christian truth, proclaimers of the true evangelical faith.

4.C.06 The Scriptures teach us that "prophetism" is es-sential to the life of the Church. The Church "prophesies" when it proclaims that the construction of the socialist so-ciety – which brings us closer to the reconstruction of the human being as a worker and "econome" and as a free and com-munity being – is a most essential part of the march of the human historical process, a march in which the achievements of the human spirit remain as concrete signs of the historic action of the Spirit in the bringing about the Kingdom.

4.C.07 The Church "prophesies" when it lives, in each one of its faithful, the triumph of love over un-love, justice over exploitation, truth over justice, peace over competition, decorum over human indignity. The Church lives "prophetically" in its members when they become committed participants in the death of the capitalist society and the dehumanizing and decrepit values it represents. Otherwise the Church would be converted into a "scandal" for God and a "reproach" for all people, and its "destruction will not be long in coming" like that of all false prophets.

4.C.08 The Church "prophesies" when its members joyfully

live the feelings and actions of growing solidarity of our
socialist people for all the peoples of the world. The Church
"prophesies" when it expresses its joy for the evident fact
that this deep feeling of solidarity is becoming a generalized
characteristic of the common citizen.

CONCLUSION

5.01 As we end this Declaration of Faith, the Presbyterian-Reformed Church in Cuba recognizes that its declared
faith can only be certain when we confidently live the truths
implicit in it.

5.01.a that this world is "God's world;"

5.01.b that Nature is the "theatre" where the human being - a creature in the "image and likeness of God" - is placed
so that s/he be a worker and an "econome;"

5.01.c that Society is the "stage" where God and God's
creature meet to be mutually realized in a concrete and eternal alliance through the implanting of Peace by the establishment of structures of Love-Justice which normalize human relations.

5.01.d that History is the "plot" of the development
and strengthening of that Alliance of Pact;

5.01.e that the Kingdom is the "unravelling of the plot"-
slowly at times and suddenly other times - with realizations
and achievements that the "plot" from time to time has, since
the Kingdom of God and God's creature are identified with
each other, because the Kingdom, Jesus Christ himself, is
the Son of God and our Older Brother.

5.02 The Presbyterian-Reformed Church in Cuba is aware
that, as it lives these truths, it comes dangerously close
to the radical secularization taken on by God in Jesus Christ,
and runs the same risks that He did of misunderstandings, sufferings and crucifixion.

5.03 Nevertheless, the Presbyterian-Reformed Church in
Cuba hopes confidently and joyfully that, as it does this, it

may become more fully a part of the glorious freedom of the
Risen One, a freedom which will free it from the alienating
ideologizations that in the past and still in the present have
kept the Church of Jesus Christ, in many aspects and in many
places, captive of the unjust and oppressive structures, of
"principalities and powers." These structures and "powers"
have made the human being an exploiter of his/her neighbor.
The Church that is not ashamed of this fact has distorted and
distorts the Gospel of Jesus Christ.

5.04 The Presbyterian-Reformed Church in Cuba hopes confidently and humbly that this liberation will capacitate it
to respond with greater effectiveness to the primary inevitable question with which God confronts all human beings
without exception: "Where is your brother/sister?"

5.05 The Presbyterian-Reformed Church in Cuba, with the
confidence and assurance that spring from the Gospel, and
only from the Gospel, looks for the concrete answer to the
divine questioning in "love that faith sets in motion," knowing, in "hope against hope," that that is the only way given
to the human being by God in Jesus Christ to find the divine
answer to his/her crucially final questions as a creature:
"Tell me your Name." "Tell me who I am."

5.06 The Presbyterian-Reformed Church in Cuba, in all
humility before its Lord and before all the people, finally
asks itself: Will we definitively come to know "Who He is"
and "Who we are" in order to be able to communicate this with
redeeming effectiveness, the sign of our evangelizing mission,
the identification of the Church? Only in the measure in
which we fulfill the concrete loving demands of Justice and
Peace which the divine interpellation imposes on us, will
we be able to satisfy the hope of really being the Church of
Jesus Christ in this world, because then "we will be like
Him," for "as He is, so are we in this world" in the fulness
of Love.

(Cuba, 1977)

*   *   *

POSTSCRIPT

While still in the process of being printed, we have received the unforeseen and tragic news of the death of Rev.
Augusto Cotto, in the Mexican press. The notice said he
died on September 24, 1980, in San Salvador.

An official statement by the Armed Forces of the Resistance (FARN) confirmed that he had "disappeared in an airplane accident off the coast of Panama while on duty." Augusto was a chaplain in the FARN and was responsible for the
International Relations for the High Command of the FARN.

Augusto Cotto was born on October 21, 1941, in Jerez,
Department of Jutiapa, Guatemala, close to the frontier of
El Salvador. As a child he was taken to San Marcos, in El
Salvador, where he studied through school and the university.

In 1964 he graduated with a degree in Theology from the
Hispanic-American Baptist Seminary in Los Angeles, Califor-
nia. He was a pastor in the Baptist Church in Santa Ana,
El Salvador, until 1969. Because of his activities in the
workers' struggles he had to leave the country and went to
Mexico. There he became a professor of ethics in the Baptist
Seminary in Mexico City. In 1971 he was elected Dean and he
became the Rector in 1974.

In 1976, in his capacity as Rector of the Baptist Seminary of Mexico, he became visiting professor in the Evangelical Seminary of Theology of Matanzas, Cuba.

Augusto was one of the founders of the Christian Movement for Peace, Independence and Progress of Peoples, which
is the name adopted in Latin America and the Caribbean for
the Christian Peace Conference. He was a member of its Committee for Continuation of Work and Associate of its Commission of Theological Studies. In the latter capacity he was
one of those responsible for the International Meeting of
Theologians entitled "Evangelization and Politics." A partial
report of that meeting is included in this book.

Comrade Cotto participated actively in other movements
and ecumenical organizations in Latin America. He was vice
president of the Association of Latin American Schools of
Theology (ALET) and up to his death he was treasurer for the
Continental Federation of Christian Students (FUMEC).

"To be a Latin American Christian," he liked to say, "is
to advance the social revolution, that is, to abolish the

present state of things and to establish another, qualita-
tively different. It is to build a new society for the new
person, based on new relationships of production. It is to
end the submission of some countries to others, of some
classes to others, of some people to others."

For Augusto Cotto these were not merely words, since
to live them, he dedicated his life to the cause of the liberation of El Salvador and Latin America. And for that cause
he died while fulfilling his Christian and revolutionary
vocation.

*   *   *

The English edition carries this tribute to Rev. Augusto
Cotto. Father Rutilio Sanchez, a priest in El Salvador, wrote
the following poem on the eve of his departure to join the
popular forces in combat against the present Salvadorean
government.

Hi, Compañeros,
My Dear Ones.

I want to let you know I'm on the road
and when you receive my letter
I will have arrived where I'm going.

I'm going into combat
I have in my napsack
a Bible,
some bullets,
a bottle full of hope,
and all the courage I can hold.

I'm going to catch up with my people
who left to go up in the mountains.
I'm going joyfully
to a new life;
I'm searching for the dawn and the new day.
I will be among friends and I'll return soon.
But one thing is certain:
I'll not return alone.
I will return with them
we will all return.

I'll not return until we return
bringing life, happiness, peace.

I think about the happiness of arriving
and being back together again like always.

Together we will fight
we will face the enemy together.

Friends, my dear ones,
I'll not return until the people return;
I'll return bringing Oscar Romero
I will return
as winter and summer return.

Alive or dead
I will return.

                                    Chema

El Salvador,
1982

          *   *   *

WHAT IS THE NEW YORK CIRCUS?

The NEW YORK CIRCUS is an ecumenical specialized ministry located in New York City. The NEW YORK CIRCUS collective joins with those searching for new definitions and directions for Christians who participate in the struggle for justice and liberation. The NEW YORK CIRCUS takes its name from the notion of tent-making ministry, a church without walls, that makes itself present in people's struggles for liberation. The work of the NEW YORK CIRCUS is focused around three main areas:

1) The NEW YORK CIRCUS ministers on a daily basis within the Latin American community and among disenfranchised working people in New York City.

2) The NEW YORK CIRCUS operates a research, documentation and action center for social justice and international awareness. Its library concentrates on the Popular Church and the Theology of Liberation.

3) The NEW YORK CIRCUS provides educational materials on the life and struggles of the contemporary church, with a primary focus on the Popular Church in Latin America.

As a part of its educational outreach, the NEW YORK CIRCUS collective has a bi-monthly publication called LUCHA/STRUGGLE. This 40-page journal carries analysis and reflection on domestic issues, international issues, focusing on Latin America, and religious issues. Frequently theological reflections and Bible studies are included, as well as analysis of the Church within the Latin American context.

We welcome requests for further information about our work and publication. In addition, upon request we would be pleased to send you a sample copy of LUCHA/STRUGGLE. The NEW YORK CIRCUS is a non-profit organization. All contributions are tax-deductible. Please direct all inquiries to:

NEW YORK CIRCUS
P.O. Box 37
Times Square Station
New York, New York 10108